FINISH WHAT YOU START AND
FEARLESSLY TAKE ON ANY GOAL

WORK ENERGY

JIM HARMER

Work Energy
Finish What You Start and Fearlessly Take On Any Goal
Income School LLC © 2020

Book Production by Aloha Publishing, AlohaPublishing.com
Interior Design by Fusion Creative Works, FusionCW.com
Softcover ISBN: 978-0-578-59998-4
Hardcover ISBN: 978-0-578-62010-7
eBook ISBN: 978-0-578-61079-5

For more information, visit IncomeSchool.com

Published by Income School

Printed in the United States of America

CONTENTS

DEDICATION (SORT OF)

This book is dedicated to the "like" button.

Okay, not the like button itself, but to those who pushed it after reading my blog posts or watching my videos over the last few years. The world is full of critics, cynics, and internet trolls, and as someone who works online, I've met plenty of them—believe me! This book is dedicated to those who have made themselves lovable and who treat others well—even when they are online.

This book is 60% story and 40% lessons learned. It includes so much story because I had to learn each lesson through experience. This will not be like every other self-development book, which seems to always start with a researcher who studied millionaires. The author then does a few interviews of said rich and successful people and *poof!* The author suddenly has an epiphany that all successful people have something in common ("There was a pattern!"). They find the key to success was X, Y, or Z. The rest of the book is filled with examples we've all heard before of famous entrepreneurs at Fortune 500 companies who fit the thesis. While I enjoy those business books, I wanted to produce something really authentic.

Your goals are personal and will impact who you become, so I owe it to you to open up about how I've taken on some of mine. I did my best not to turn this book into one long "humblebrag," but this is a goals book after all, so forgive me. I can't teach you how to be outgoing or eloquent or any of the other things with which I struggle. I certainly can't teach you how to cook. But I can teach you how to crush every goal in your path. That's what I do.

One of my goals has been to create an online business to support my family. As I've done that, I've recognized and developed a *work energy* formula that largely created my success. I've applied it to many other goals now and it is the key. As you read this story and apply the work energy formula, you will quickly find the confidence to fearlessly take on any goal.

> *Work energy is the personal inner drive that makes you tick.*

It is the unique mechanism your mind has developed to get things done, and it has been shaped by your life's experience. While you may apply your work energy to a career, the word "work" refers to the work you must put in to achieve a goal.

One more thing before we begin. I've learned after years of having over a million people follow me on social media that no matter how loud the trolls sound, the best route is for me to always be my authentic self—even when there are those who don't like who I am. So, in this book, I will tell the story as I lived it. I'll mention briefly my religious beliefs where they fit into the story, politics, my distaste for MLMs, and why I hate fish sticks.

If any of those parts of who I am will hurt your feelings, turn back now before it's too late. Head for the hills! Otherwise, let's begin a story that I have told to only a few—a story that will help you crush your goals.

Crap. I've already messed this book up. The dedication is supposed to be a warmhearted thank-you to someone you love, and now I'm turning it into a disclaimer about how offended you're gonna be by reading this book. I hope you'll give me a break—I'm new to this. Blog posts don't require dedications.

FOREWORD

Ten years ago, when I started ImprovePhotography.com, I could never have imagined that eventually its pages would be visited more than 72 million times. An entire 0.6% of the world's population came to Improve Photography at some point in the last decade. That's a rather ridiculous statistic—nobody gets excited about achieving only 0.6% of anything positive.

"Woo! I lost 0.6% of a pound!"

"Boom! I got a 0.6% return in the stock market this year!"

"Ma! I got a 0.6% on my test!"

But in this case, I'm absolutely amazed by it. That's because 0.6% of the entire planet came to my little blog I created largely while eating Cheez-Its and wearing pajamas.

The reach of social media and websites is incredible. Every Monday I sit down on a chair and talk to a camera for 10 minutes. I upload the file to YouTube and 30,000 people watch it (sometimes many more).

That's amazing to me because as I sit here writing this, I am typing on my wife's aging Macbook Air with a horrendously dirty screen (does she really spit *that much* when she talks?), wearing basketball shorts and a T-shirt, and I have bedhead. Oh, and let's just set a tone of perfect honesty right here from the beginning of this story: I might also add that I have a bit of a nasty smell on me right now because I haven't even showered for the morning. Yep, that's me. Yet the incredible reach of the internet has attracted four out of every 100 English-speaking people on planet Earth— from Russia to Brazil to China to the United States—to my little blog.

Sheesh. The dedication turned into a disclaimer about how offensive this book would be, and now this foreword is getting a little braggy.

Hold it.

I'm also pretty sure that you're not supposed to write your own foreword. A foreword is supposed to be written by someone famous and important who barely knows you, but who you pay to write it so it will seem to the reader like you are friends. Let's just pretend that this entire section was written by Ellen DeGeneres, with input from Gandhi.

Okay. That's really quite enough. Let's just skip these obligatory sections in "real" books and start the story about how you can crush your goals. You'll like it better—I promise.

PART I

THE WORK ENERGY FORMULA

1

COLD FISH STICKS

> *"To each there comes in their lifetime a special moment when they are figuratively tapped on the shoulder and offered the chance to do a very special thing, unique to them and fitted to their talents. What a tragedy if that moment finds them unprepared or unqualified for that which could have been their finest hour."*
> *—Sir Winston Churchill*

If on July 7, 2009, at around midnight, you would have driven down Pine Ridge Road in Naples, Florida, and stopped in at the dollar store, you would have found me in the back wearing a ragged apron, with headphones in and paper cuts on a couple fingers, as I stocked the shelves for nearly minimum wage. It was the only job I could get. I had a newly minted bachelor's degree on the wall, yet I was stocking shelves for a few dollars per hour.

Every night after work I came home around 3 a.m., frustrated to no end, feeling like an abject failure, and fell on my knees. My prayers mostly went like this in those days:

"Please make this come to an end. I need a better job so I can take care of Emily and the baby. Amen."

Improving our situation was about the only thing I could focus on (although, in retrospect, I wish I would have relaxed a bit and taken my family to the Florida beaches more often).

Maybe your goals have felt like that. There are some things you easily accomplish, but there are others that seem to haunt you. Goals that always seem outside your grasp. Problems that you know you need to solve but that your best efforts never do. I've been there, and this story will help you to know how to change it.

It was in these days that I learned what "soul-grinding work" felt like. I despised every instant of work at the dollar store. I remember being so transfixed on how inefficient the system of getting the product on the shelves was that I could barely pay attention to my work.

I'm not from Florida. Emily and I had been married for two years. Our son, Ruger, was still such a little baby that he couldn't even roll over yet. Just a few months before this dollar store torture began we had lived in rural Idaho.

How It Started

I attended Brigham Young University-Idaho in Rexburg. I received a degree in Communications and got a very generous scholarship to law school in Florida. I had a wonderful family, and I was going to be on the beach soaking up the sun with a law book in my hand for the next three years. What seemed too perfect in planning turned out so imperfect in reality.

I arrived in Florida a few days before Emily did so I could find somewhere to live, somewhere to work, and something to drive. We sold literally everything we owned that wouldn't fit into one of our three suitcases, but we didn't care. We were so happy to be going places in life that nothing else mattered.

I had everything planned out meticulously. I had done months of research on starting salaries for lawyers, how much law school would cost, how much it would cost to buy a car and live in Naples during school—details! My Excel sheet was king, and no contingency was left unaccounted for.

I spent two days driving my rental car around this wonderful new tropical paradise, looking up Craigslist ads for used cars. I finally found a reliable, used hunter-green sedan for sale by a man named José. I inspected the car carefully, went on a test drive, and everything looked great. I plunked down $5,000 cash and signed the title just minutes before heading off to the airport to pick up Emily and Ruger.

I rolled down the windows as I drove the 20 minutes to the airport, whizzing past palm trees and smelling Florida's warm, humid air. Coldplay's "Viva La Vida" was the new song on the radio. Then it was back to Naples with the family as I pointed out all of the great things I'd found in the city already.

It was Emily and me against the whole world.

Driving down Goodlette-Frank Road, you guessed it, *ca-CLUNK!* The engine revved as I pressed the gas pedal, yet there was no acceleration. Looking ahead, I spied the yellow sign for Gulf Coast Transmission on my right and we literally rolled on momentum into the parking lot. Perfect placement for a transmission shop, by the way. Just like in the movies, we coasted into the mechanic's shop. It was a beautifully cinematic way to see a car die, and the theatrics were not lost on me.

An older gentleman looked at the car and, in his thick German accent, informed me that the transmission was broken. Frustrated, but still riding high, I said, "Okay, how long will it take to fix? How much will it cost me?" Those of you who know anything about cars just laughed, realizing that a transmission is no simple fix. I'll include here a full and complete list of everything I know how to do with a car: drive it, put windshield washer fluid in it, and check the oil.

Consequently, the German mechanic's message didn't translate into my brain. I could see he was frustrated with me, and so he spoke more simply for my simple mind. "The fix costs more than the car. Kaput!"

Ah, now this I understood. Three years of high school German finally paid off. Kaput equals broken. Basically, this man thoughtfully explained to me that my car wasn't working.

This was something I already knew. Surely this car, the product of intensive research, could be repaired for the right price. I spoke in the simplest words I could so that he would understand: "Yes, it is kaput. How much to un-kaput?"

With growing frustration, he said, "Transmission kaput, cheap crappy car that you shouldn't have bought in the first place is also kaput."

He also kindly took the time to show me how the seller had rigged the car to temporarily run well on a test drive, and how it was obvious to any mechanic that the car was circling the drain. Got it. Basically, I led my family into a disaster 2,500 miles away from home.

The guy who sold me the car got my $5,000, and I got a lesson in how the world worked outside the bubble of the small, very religious town I came from.

The tow guy taught me the next lesson in foolishly trusting people. Tell us the tow is $200, but then make it $200 for both coming to pick up the car *and* $200 to drive back home afterward. Seriously, tow guy, that was genius. I totally didn't see that life lesson coming either. By that point, I felt so defeated that I didn't even argue with the dishonest tow-truck driver. I just didn't have any fight left in me.

Excel sheet—busted. Apparently, there *were* contingencies I hadn't planned for.

It took a few hours for the reality of the situation to sink in, but life had placed a mountain of a problem in front of me. I knew my next goal in life would be the most challenging yet—to reach financial independence. What I didn't yet know was that life was about to kick me while I was down.

We stayed at the cheapest hotel we could find that night. Emily put on her positive attitude that has carried us through many struggles. I suggested we go to Walmart to buy our son a $20 bouncer since we had no crib for him. We did and then came back to the hotel to put our tiny baby in this wonderfully plush, safe little place to sleep for the night, entirely unaware of his parents' worries.

As soon as we opened the box for the bouncer, we were met with a new contingency. Someone had pooped in it and returned it to the store. Right there, in the center of the bouncer, was a load of human poop. I applaud you, random pooper, for the prank on these new parents who were getting an education in how life works. Never again have I purchased anything that was previously pooped on. It was as if the entire planet was bent on wringing out every ounce of pride we had left that day.

We were exhausted, but when we put our son back to sleep in the car seat, we opened up our other splurge from the store. On sale that day was a large bag of frozen fish sticks for about $5. We reasoned that it was the largest quantity of food we could purchase for that amount of money, so we bought it.

Hungry and exhausted, we opened up the bag and looked about our room to find the microwave, only to see an empty wall. For two days, we gnawed on thawing fish sticks until we were certain they had gone bad—because there was no fridge either.

As the morning light filtered through the curtains, Emily woke up with a fever and sore throat. It lasted for days and we knew it was strep. Another $350 at urgent care later, she was on the mend.

All of our careful planning was entirely undone in the space of 24 hours.

We were down and out, but we always knew we had family who would help us if we let them know of our situation. We did, and my parents stepped in to help us get an inexpensive but reliable car. I am grateful that both Emily's parents and mine made safe financial decisions for so many years. Because of it, we've always been cared for.

We now had a basic car, and we found a little apartment.

Yet the digits on the Excel file continued to dwindle. I had to find a summer job before school, and fast. The trouble was it was summer in a city whose businesses came to a screeching halt when the snowbirds went back to Vermont. Oh, and it was 2009. Even fast-food restaurants wouldn't take my application when I informed them I would only be able to work there for the remaining five months before the school year.

Weeks went by before I finally got an interview at a women's shoe store in the mall. I guess I wasn't a good fit because the teenage girl who managed the store never called back. Then I got a call from a dollar store. I dressed in my best to put on a good face for the interview—ready with my resume on which I'd bolded the parts about having a bachelor's degree, speaking two languages, being a student body officer in college, and experience running a small business.

The manager, who was only a couple of years older than me, looked up and down the resume for a long time as I sat awkwardly waiting. Finally, he looked up and said, with a face showing obvious disappointment for what I'd become in life, "You don't have any experience at all in stocking shelves. What makes you think you could make it here?"

Excuse me? Make it here? I had a college degree and this guy thought I might not have the mental capacity to understand the complexities of opening up boxes and putting the probably-pooped-on products on the shelves?

Somehow, I convinced him to give me a shot, and I was issued an apron and a box cutter. I'd report to work by 11 p.m. and clock out at 3 a.m. each weekday.

I was humbled, but I was grateful to have whatever paycheck I could get to provide for my wife and child. Every night I'd fret over going to work, hate every instant of my job, and come home exhausted. The work was so painfully dull that I had to have a distraction.

The path toward my goal was about to begin, and I didn't realize it.

Since we had paid our way through college buying and flipping things on Craigslist, we scoured our three suitcases to find anything we could possibly sell for a little extra cash. We had only two valuable possessions: an iPod Shuffle that Emily's dad had given her and an inexpensive Canon Rebel XS digital camera. Our net worth? About $300.

About six months prior, I'd bought the camera when I was nervous about becoming a father of a newborn. I thought photography would be a fun hobby for a dad, so I sold my skis and a gun to purchase the camera. It was a stretch to spend $500 on *anything*, but I had earned the money and we had our needs met at the time, so I went for it.

As I began making the Craigslist post for the camera, Emily saw what I was doing and *begged* me not to sell it. She said she couldn't bear to see me part with it, even though we were in need, when I'd worked so hard to earn it and enjoyed it so much. Reluctantly, I kept it.

As it would turn out, Emily's insistence that we keep my camera would earn us millions of dollars over the next few years and entirely change our lives.

One of the few possessions we also kept was her iPod Shuffle, which was still pretty cool in those days. A little rectangle that could make hundreds of songs come out of it was still quite a novelty. I guess listening to music trumped having food because I started bringing the iPod to work with me so I would have a distraction from the boredom.

Because I was a nerd, I knew about podcasts, but to most people, they were still a foreign concept. I downloaded every free podcast I could find— tips for law students, religion, news, politics, and even business podcasts. That's when one of the podcasts mentioned a new website called "Smart Passive Income" by Pat Flynn.

He didn't have a podcast yet, but I found some free software that could make PDFs of his blog posts. Then I found another piece of software that could convert PDFs into an mp3 file with a horribly mechanical voice reading the text to me.

I downloaded everything—every word—every day.

He shared things like how he had started a website and made money selling an ebook study guide to people who visited the site.

I also listened to podcasts like *Internet Business Mastery* and a dozen others. They were earning real money online by creating websites and podcasts to gather an audience. Then they made money selling online courses and having advertising on their sites. I was riveted.

Every night, I listened to every business and technology podcast I could find as I repeatedly put cans on shelves. My shift would end, and I'd get home just before the horizon would begin to light up with color.

On my knees each morning before I crashed into bed, I'd plead for God to help me find a better job until school started—anything! I didn't understand why we had to go through that hardship, and I certainly didn't realize that the answer to my prayers was the hardship itself.

> *The answer to my prayers was the hardship itself.*

I just wanted to find a better temporary job or stumble upon a pile of money on the street. Surely God could arrange for that. Instead, I received something far greater—endless hours at a dull job with no distractions, where my headphones brought the best minds of the new world of blogging and business right to my earbuds. I had months and months of the most knowledgeable people in internet business tutoring me every single night, and I didn't even appreciate what I was receiving.

Sometimes God's greatest gifts really are "unanswered prayers." Thank you, Garth Brooks.

This book is about fearlessly taking on any goal you can dream up, but for most people, career and financial goals are often at the fore. In the ensuing decade, I have worked with thousands of people wanting to start their own small businesses. It's a massive goal, and this book will teach you the *work energy formula* for taking it on.

Others of you want to achieve health, familial, or other goals. Perhaps you just want to excel at the job you already have. A Harris Interactive study found that only 20% of American workers report feeling "very passionate" about their jobs. At first glance, that statistic may not seem dire. Sure, only 20% of workers are "very passionate" about their jobs, but many others at least don't despise their work, right? Not so fast. A study by Gallup[1] found that only 15% of employees are engaged in their work.

Just think of what those numbers mean. If you are like most people today, you are not engaged or passionate about the place you will spend eight hours a day for decades of your life. Will you be satisfied with your life if that's how you spend so much of it?

Worse yet, what about the time after work? If you don't get fulfillment from your day job and then you go home to watch TV, you'll end up wishing you were the kind of person with a passion for something—anything! You'll yearn for hobbies or some other goal you can take on and tackle. If you don't get fulfillment from something, your happiness will suffer. Whether your goal is career related or something else entirely, you must have mountains to climb if you want to be happy.

You may or may not be in the kind of job I was in, where you felt your soul was being ground into a pulp during every moment of every shift, but you probably know what that feels like, right? Most of us have, at some point, worked in a soul-grinding job. If you are in a job that is simply toxic to your being and you see no hope of change, then do yourself and your employer a favor by working on a goal to find different work. Trust me, your employer already isn't happy with your work if you feel that way.

The more likely situation, though, is that you're in a job you are glad to have. You may even like the nature of the work or the industry you're in, but statistics say that it's likely you frequently feel disengaged at work. You may even feel "passionate" about the type of work you do, but not quite to the point of feeling "very passionate." You know there's no fire in your bones driving you anymore.

If you are 35 years old today and you work a typical American workweek until retirement at an average age of 62, you'll spend another 63,168 hours at work. Just imagine sitting down on the couch and turning on an incredibly boring show like Star Trek and watching it over and over for the next 7.2 years without sleeping, eating, or going to the bathroom. That's how much time you'll spend at work. Depending on your job, Star Trek may be a generous metaphor. Some people have jobs so bad that it would be more like watching Major League Baseball. Can. You. Imagine?

What would your personality, happiness, and outlook be like after 7.2 years of this torture? That's what you're doing to your life, if you continue doing soul-grinding work for an entire career. You owe it to the people who love and need you, as well as to yourself, to find work you love. I don't care if that work is being a fancy financial analyst or painting houses—you need to love it. Most of you reading this book don't need a new position at a new company. You need a new fire within yourself to love what you once thought was the best place for you to work. You picked your job, so let's fix whatever has you feeling dispassionate.

Achieving your goals is not entirely about the work you do in the course of your employment, although that certainly applies. Stay-at-home moms, retirees, and every other breathing person need to feel that they are working toward something, or life will have little meaning.

I'm going to get you fired up. Once you understand the work energy formula, you'll have a fire in your bones that you can turn on and wield as a weapon against any goal before you. I'm confident that as you follow my story about how I learned, step-by-step, to overcome obstacles, be fearless in any setting, and achieve the most difficult goals, you'll be able to develop that same ability.

Soul-Grinding Work Is Not One Size Fits All

First, though, we must understand why some work feels like drudgery to you when that same task may be enjoyable to others. Why was the dollar store work soul grinding to me when others enjoyed working there for decades? The ability to reach your goals won't do you any good if they take you in the wrong direction.

If you can identify the soul-grinding work in your life, it will show you the barricades before you.

> Barricades *are types of work that conflict with your inner drive, your work energy.*

You can surely improve upon these weak areas over time, but in this book, you will simply learn to avoid them. Losing weight, getting a promotion, writing a book, stopping smoking, or paying off your house are already difficult goals to achieve. The point of this book is to show you how you can achieve those goals by using your unique inner drive: your work energy.

If you are a manager or business owner, it is critical to understand your employees' barricades as well. I spent a morning with one of my employees, going through the material in this chapter, and it revealed to me a very different approach that I need to use in designing an atmosphere where he can perform at his best.

Years into my blogging business, I hired over 50 short-term employees in just six months. They mass-produced blog posts on several sites at once, but the quality of the articles was poor despite my efforts to train them.

I theorized that I could improve the quality of the articles they were writing if I could get a few of the employees writing better content so as to inspire the others. To make it fun, I created two teams of three for each shift. The workers on these teams would go into a separate room of the office to do their work. They'd have more time to work on the articles, and I spoiled them to make it a privilege to be on the "black team." I provided them free snacks and drinks, cushy chairs, and I designed the room with a huge 10-foot flag with a custom Viking logo for the "Black Team Content Warriors." There was even a sign on the door to that room that read, "Top Secret. Black Team Only." This was one of my finest ideas ever.

It was a competition to achieve "black team" status. Each Monday, I would review the work from the two black teams and pick a winner. The winning black team would get to stay for the next week's competition, and the losing black team would go back to being regular workers and the shift would come up with three new people to be their black team for the week.

After the first week, I reviewed the articles. They were no better than the articles from the regular workers, who had much less time to write their pieces. I was frustrated, but I gave some training pointers, selected a winning team for the week, and then the next week's competition began.

This pattern continued for a few weeks until I got a call from the office manager. He had a question. "What do I do if nobody wants to be on the black team? Should I just pick some people and force them?"

My jaw hit the floor. How could they not *want* to be in the room with the cushy chairs, a more relaxed pace with nobody micro-managing them, and all the Nutter Butters and cold diet root beer they could drink? How could they not *want* to be in the room with the 10-foot flag and the custom-designed Viking logo?

The manager's answer was very simple. They didn't like the competition. They were nervous about being criticized and losing. Whose fault was it? Mine. I had designed work following my own work energy, which will be discussed later. I would have been excited about an opportunity to stand out from the crowd and receive praise in a competitive environment. The fear of criticism wouldn't have deterred me. Yet, for others, it was a barricade. I had designed the project for myself without considering the barricades of my workforce. The black team was scuttled, and I still have the flag hanging in my office to remind me of my mistake.

You need to understand the barricades in yourself, and in those around you, so that you can design a path toward a goal in a way that will not conflict with their individual needs.

For me, soul-grinding work provides me with no opportunities to take on new and difficult tasks. Repetition is my barricade. Repetition is problematic for me because it means I have to do something I have done before, so there's no challenge.

Action Step One: What Is Your Soul-Grinding Work?

What's the Worst Job You Ever Had?

First, start with your career. Think through every job you've had. What did you like about each job? What tasks required to do the job were soul grinding for you?

What about your current work? Focus on the specific tasks you have to do and not the job as a whole.

Next, think through chores you need to do around the home. What can you just not bring yourself to do? I understand that no one enjoys cleaning toilets because it's gross, but what tasks make you feel as if you're losing your soul?

With the answers to these simple questions, we're starting to understand you from the standpoint of what you dislike. Sometimes that's the best insight into understanding you as a person and identifying what makes you tick.

Think back through your whole life now. What other work was soul grinding? When have you felt that, and why did you feel it?

As an avid reader of books, I have to admit that 100% of the time, when the author asks me to reflect on a question or write something down, I skip it. I get a little grin on my face as I sneakily just keep reading, knowing the author will never catch me. I'm a rebel. So I've created a helpful resource for you, in case you do the same thing.

For now just go on your merry way reading the book, but when you get home tonight and can sit down with your spouse or someone who knows you well, go to WorkEnergyBook.com and you'll find a helpful list of these questions that you can read on your phone or print. You'll learn things about yourself you have never realized, and it will dramatically change your ability to crush your goals.

Just like those annoying radio ads, I'll repeat that one more time: Read on for now, but when you get home tonight, go to WorkEnergyBook.com. You'll get a free list of the action steps, which you can read on your phone or in print.

Once you see a clear picture of what soul-grinding work is to you, it is essential that you clearly identify your barricade. For me, working at the dollar store was soul-grinding because the tasks were so simple that I could never be praised for doing the work. My barricade is doing a task that I won't receive praise for accomplishing.

Your barricade is unique to you. I have a friend whose barricade is the kind of work where he is likely to be criticized by others. My wife's barricade is the type of work that puts her on a fixed schedule with specific deadlines.

My business partner's barricade is a task that would make him vulnerable to appearing unprepared because, deep down inside, he's afraid of looking dumb.

Once you have identified where you have suffered through soul-grinding work, look for the barricade—what about that work did you dread? Then put it into a simple phrase. What is your barricade?

2

IDENTIFY YOUR WORK ENERGY

> *"The heights by great men reached and kept were not attained by sudden flight, but they, while their companions slept, were toiling upward in the night."*
> —Henry Wadsworth Longfellow

Now that you understand the barricades that would stop your progress toward a goal, we need to turn our attention to the opposite—your work energy. *Work energy* is the personal inner drive that makes you tick. It is the unique mechanism your mind has developed to get things done. It has been shaped by your life's experience.

I discovered my own work energy when law school began after the longest summer of my life, stocking shelves at the dollar store and listening to business podcasts.

I was relieved on my last day at the dollar store, but I traded its boredom for law school's mental rigor. Each day, I woke up and headed straight for the law library to begin studying. Part of my law school dues likely went to a certain blue chair in the law library that I single-handedly wore out as I sat in it for many hours every single day.

I set a firm rule that I'd quit working at school and go home every day at 5 p.m. to spend time with family. At 5 p.m., no matter what, I was done. That served our family well and provided me with at least some time with Emily and our son, Ruger.

By day, I sat in that blue wingback chair—staring at the eight-inch screen of my horrendous $120 refurbished Dell netbook computer. Side note:

27

netbooks were the most horrid idea the tech world has ever had. I had to squint so hard to see both of the pixels on the screen that my wife says it put a permanent wrinkle between my eyes. At 5 p.m. each day, I'd ride my bike through the palm-tree-lined streets to be at home with my wonderful wife and child on the beach.

After that, I should have gone to sleep to prepare for another early start the next morning, but I had a nightly ritual. As soon as Emily and Ruger were asleep each night, I'd slip out the front door with a backpack containing the Canon Rebel XS camera and a simple tripod.

I fell in love with photography on the beaches each night, as I felt the warm, humid ocean breezes. More than a few times the police would catch me and kick me off the beach, since it closed at 10 p.m. All of the legal cases I read were stories of people trying to destroy one another's lives. But, on the beach late at night with my camera, I could hear the intermittent crashing of waves on the sand as I became a passionate hobbyist photographer. Night photography became my obsession. It fascinated me that I could go into nature at night needing a flashlight to walk around, and I could record the light with a shutter speed of 30 seconds or more and entirely expose the scene. I was enamored.

Although I was constantly under stress at school, and Emily was exhausted from taking care of the baby all day, we were generally quite happy. We spent evenings watching our little son learn how to walk, pushing him on swings, sitting on the beach, and fishing until sunset.

The situation was not easy on Emily either. She's from a very small town in Idaho and had always lived near family. Now, she was in a strange place without a friend or family member to support her. She had no money and spent all day, every day with our baby, going to parks and taking him to the library. She was emotionally drained yet had to be the one to keep us positive as I focused on law school.

We had *no* extra money. When I say we had no extra money, some of you may have the wrong idea. Some people say they are poor but have a smartphone, a reliable car, and have seen the inside of a restaurant at some point in the last 30 days. We were the *other* kind of poor. Not a true third-world-country type of poverty, but the kind where you don't fit into the society around you. I'll explain this type of poor with an example. There was a city about 30 minutes away from where we lived—a really neat little beach town that we always wanted to visit. We only went once in two years. Why? Because it was too expensive to drive 30 minutes if we didn't need to go there. During law school, we ate at restaurants about five times in three years, and each of those was when the vendors at school gave us a gift card.

To provide for our family, I applied to the adult education program put on by Collier County Parks and Recreation. There, I could teach photography classes at night at the local high school to a class of mostly retirees. In the application for the job, I had nothing to put under the "experience" line since, quite frankly, I didn't really have any experience in photography other than my nights on the beach. Yet Tay Baker, who surely doesn't remember me, approved my application and said he'd let me try it out. He'll likely never know how his decision to give me a chance at teaching that photography class once a week would change the course of my life.

On Tuesday nights at 8 p.m., I taught my class of 20-30 people about the basics of photography. I was hardly an expert. I just shared the information I'd learned over the last year and a half of being a hobbyist photographer. The members of the class were good to me and seemed to enjoy the class.

Every six weeks, I'd get a new group of students. After three or four sessions of my course, I realized I was answering the same questions over and over. I'd explain aperture, ISO, and shutter speed, and then six weeks later, I had a new group of students whom I had to teach the same thing.

That's when I decided to start ImprovePhotography.com. The blog began as a way to communicate with my class. I would write tutorials there, and when someone asked a question I'd answered previously, I could direct them to the article.

I honestly can't say if I created the site to merely communicate with my class, or if I also wondered if I could build traffic on that site and turn it into a business. If I did think about how I could build it up, it was a dream I didn't quite dare communicate to anyone.

Those long nights at the dollar store had become useful. From the podcasts I'd listened to while working there, I had learned about WordPress, how to write for the web, plugins, and SEO (search engine optimization). All of it came out naturally when I started my website—despite the fact that I was really just communicating with the couple dozen students in my class.

I installed software that allowed me to see a map on the back end of my website. It displayed an orange dot on a world map every time someone visited my site in real time. I could see when someone accessed my site, and approximately where in the world they were.

My first blog posts were bad in a way you can probably imagine from a 24-year-old, first-time blogger who had only purchased his first real camera a few months previous. Yet I focused on sharing the things I'd learned so far and tried to be helpful to the people in my photography night class in Florida. When they asked what an aperture was, I would write an answer on the site so I wouldn't have to explain the concept to a later class.

While I am a capable writer, writing is not one of my gifts. I was never talented in creative writing or developing stories. However, I found the process of writing blog posts refreshingly easy. I had always been able to explain things simply to people, and I wrote the words I would have spoken. Blogging didn't require rigid grammatical rules or structured writing forms like the writing I had to do during college.

I published a few articles each week on my blog but was mostly focused on the potential of building a local audience of photographers to whom I could sell photography workshops outside of class.

Yet, every few days, I saw an orange dot appear on the map, showing that someone from around the world had visited one of my site's pages. Initially, all of those dots came from Naples, Florida, where I lived. They began to spread. Something about the map captivated me. I stared at that map like most people stare at a TV. I'd squint at both of my netbook's pixels and, sure enough, every few hours, a new dot would pop up.

After a couple months, the dots began to come more regularly, and from all around the world. Google had found my site and was starting to show my little disaster of a blog to more people. I'd have to wait 15 or 20 minutes sometimes before another dot would appear, but it brought a sense of fascination.

A New Obsession Beyond Photography

I remember seeing one week that 100 people had visited the site. Given that I only had 20 students, it was an electrifying discovery. I began to make writing on the website a daily exercise and readjusted my focus to writing for the world at large and not just the students in my class.

It only took a few months before I saw orange dots popping up quickly—from all over the globe. At this point, I didn't have a strategy. I didn't know the first thing about SEO, link building, or how to drive traffic to a site. I had no idea how to do keyword research to find out what articles would bring the most traffic to the site, or what type of article would rank better on search engines. That felt like a limitation at the time, but looking back now with years more experience, I was actually doing more right than wrong.

I learned how to drive traffic from watching the orange dots appear for so many years. I'd write an article, put it out there, and then watch how many dots popped up for people reading the article. I saw, in a very practical sense, what worked. And I quickly learned that I had my best success from the extremely long articles with tons of information. A lot of people think short, easy blog posts are best, but years of running experience shows me the opposite.

The second lesson I learned is that if I wanted to bring people to my website, I had to focus on what *they* wanted, instead of what I wanted them to know. When you write a textbook, you have a captive audience and can teach whatever you want. When you write a blog post and hope someone will find it, you have to write the answer to the question they type in Google. You have to answer people's questions.

As the orange dots began to appear with greater regularity, the overall numbers piled up. In April 2011, I had 855 pageviews on the website. While that number is tiny by today's standards, it was incredibly exciting to me back then.

Instead of picturing 855 pageviews as a very small website, I thought about it differently. There were 20 people in my night class on photography. I was willing to prepare a lesson, drive to the high school, and teach a class to just 20 people. Yet 855 people read what I wrote on my blog! I pictured an auditorium with 855 people in it. If I were asked to give a speech to 855 people, I'd be honored! So why would I have any less enthusiasm for my little blog?

I decided it was time to create a product to sell to the 855 people on my website, something that could be useful and accessed around the world. Just days before I made this decision, Steve Jobs stood on a stage in California and announced the "iPad." It had been rumored for over a year, and while there were laughs when Steve Jobs gave it the name of a feminine hygiene product, the lines stacked up in front of stores as millions of people rushed to buy. I was not one of them because I was flat broke. You remember—the *other* kind of broke. But I was intrigued by what opportunities it would create.

One of the new opportunities was digital books. eBooks were already in existence, but this pushed them to the forefront. I was about to become an author.

I had no experience in internet marketing or writing a book, but the podcasts I listened to kept mentioning ebooks as a new opportunity. So, I got to work. I opened up a Word document and started typing everything I'd learned about photography over the last year and a half. At this point, I was an intermediate photographer. I felt like a charlatan writing a book, but I wanted to share the things I had learned so far, and I realized that if I did not hold myself out to be an expert by my tone in the book, I could make it work.

I set a goal to have my book published in two weeks, from start to finish. The next morning, I awoke before the sun and began typing until it was time for school. As I rode the mile on my bike to the law school, my mind raced with ideas of what I could put into my ebook.

I accomplished little in school for the next two weeks. I sat near the back of the lecture hall and opened my book to a random page and pretended to be taking notes as I filled my outdated netbook with everything I had learned about photography. That strategy worked quite well most of the time, as I was ahead in my studies.

It worked less well in torts. A tort is a non-contract wrongful act that brings about civil liability. Every law student takes torts class in their first year of legal studies. To protect myself from a crushing defamation lawsuit that would certainly ruin me, we'll call the teacher Professor Jones. She was actually a very nice lady, but in the classroom, she was fierce and by far the smartest person in the room.

All law school courses are taught using the Socratic method. This means that students read the material before class, and then the professor badgers individual students with questions to test their knowledge and deepen their understanding. With some of the professors, this frankly wasn't an intimidating prospect as they'd throw out softball questions.

In Professor Jones's class, however, we were all petrified. The woman was an expert at the Socratic method. I swear she spent all night dreaming of ways to make pretentious law students cry the following morning. Some people read the news while eating breakfast; she selected her victims in her head.

There were approximately 80 students in the classroom on the day I started working on my book. I sat on the far right side of the classroom against the wall, which was my first mistake. Never let Professor Jones think you're afraid.

Still, doing the math, there were 80 students and she'd likely only pick five to grill that day. Math was on my side, so I took a calculated risk.

The class began with a five-minute soliloquy by Professor Jones on the finer points of tort law. Then, it began.

"Mr. Oakey, will you please tell us the facts of Palsgraf v. Long Island Railroad?" Excellent, I thought. Now there are 79 students left and only four more people will be grilled. Five percent chance? I'll take it. I continued tapping out my ebook as poor Mr. Oakey stood and recited the facts of Palsgraf before the executioner.

"Okay . . . uh . . . So there is this lady named Helen Palsgraf who is taking her daughters to the beach in 1924. Two guys try to jump on the train in front of Palsgraf and a railroad employee helps the second one to step up. Trouble is that one of them has a suitcase full of fireworks. The fireworks fall and explode, causing the railroad's heavy metal scale to fall over and hit

Ms. Palsgraf. She sues the railroad, arguing that it was negligent in assisting the man to get on the train who then dropped the fireworks."

They had just gotten through the facts of the case. Next was a rundown of the issue, then the rule of law, and then any dissenting opinions. I had at least another 10 minutes to work on my ebook, as I completely missed out on learning from one of the most famous legal cases of all time. I glanced up just as I saw Professor Jones's eyes sweep over to mine. I instantly knew I was in for it. I had one of those "I have no idea what's going on" looks in my eyes, and she could smell blood in the water.

"Mr. Harmer, what was the ruling in the case?" Oh, crud. I am Mr. Harmer. I stood up to take my beating. I had read the case, but this was the first time I'd come to class without detailed notes prepared. I flipped open my book in a hurry as I stood up and saw blank margins—not a single note.

"Uh . . . the issue, in this case, is that it was the fireworks of another passenger that hurt the plaintiff. It wasn't the railroad employee who did it."

"Oh, how nice. But I asked what the finding was, not the issue."

"Well, I . . . I know the defendant didn't win. There was a dissent, but I know the plaintiff didn't recover."

"How nice. You've discovered the holding. Now, why isn't the railroad responsible?"

"Well, the railroad didn't light the fireworks. It was the other customer's fireworks that blew up—not the railroad's fireworks."

She wasn't letting go. "Yes, but the fireworks didn't hurt the plaintiff. It was the railroad's scale that tipped over and hurt the plaintiff. So didn't the railroad cause the harm to the plaintiff?"

"Well, yes . . . but . . . " I madly looked through my empty page in my book searching for the answer " . . . I . . . "

Professor Jones: "Well, let's see if there's someone in the class who actually studied the case . . . "

Ouch. She moved on to her next victim, and after a few minutes, the sting of the embarrassment dulled enough that I could turn my attention back to my ebook on the basics of photography. About every other day, this scene would repeat itself. I'd be working my brains out trying to write the book, and every once in a while I'd get a metaphorical punch in the gut by a professor who wanted to remind me that I was still a law student.

Oh, and in case you're wondering, Palsgraf didn't get any money because the harm was not foreseeable. The employee could not have foreseen that, as he helped the customer, another customer could be injured by fireworks that he didn't know existed. He couldn't have foreseen that his suitcase would explode and cause a chain reaction of harm to someone else. Palsgraf was out of luck.

Day after day, this embarrassing situation repeated itself as I focused more on writing my ebook than on law school. "Mr. Harmer, what is the eggshell plaintiff rule?" Um . . .

Think about what was happening: I put my family through hell so I could go to law school. I spent an entire year studying for the exam to get in. I was willing to be the *other* kind of broke to go to law school. I actually enjoyed law school. Yet there was something about working on the blog that was so fascinating I was perfectly willing to set law school aside for weeks at a time to work on it.

> *Your work energy is so compelling to your spirit that it is nearly impossible to shut off once you've tapped into it.*

This is so important to understand that it bears repeating: There is a powerful fountain of motivation inside of you. You have felt it before—even if at fleeting moments throughout your life. It can push you to climb any mountain and destroy any problem in your path.

In the action step for this chapter, you'll discover what your individual work energy is.

My work energy drove me to write that ebook. I was so committed to the work that I produced an entire 30,000-word book in two weeks, while doing law school full time and also holding two part-time jobs. It didn't require tremendous self-discipline. I had an itch and my work energy begged me to scratch it. I couldn't focus on anything else.

After a few days, I figured out how to format my Word document for e-readers, and my book went live. I couldn't figure out how to make it so that when someone bought it, it would automatically give them the download, so every time I saw a sale I'd just send them an email manually and attach the product.

In the first few days, I sold a couple dozen books. Then, I had an idea. I would call in to Leo Laporte's *Tech Guy Podcast* and ask him a question about creating an ebook, and then off-handedly mention that my book was available for sale.

I waited on the phone for over two hours but then all of a sudden, I was talking to the famous Leo Laporte. I had spent two hours on hold practicing exactly how I'd word my question, and as soon as I went live on the air, my blood ran cold and I could barely force the words out of my lips. I stammered through my question—something about PDF permissions—and made sure to mention my book and website. I'm certain that Leo saw right through me and realized I was just trying to get a free ad, but he was extremely gracious about it. He answered my question and allowed me to mention my book. I owe him something because I really needed the little confidence boost I got from mentioning my book on his radio show.

Over the next 45 minutes after mentioning the book on his show, I sold over $300 worth of PDF ebooks. I spent the next two days obsessively refreshing my PayPal account, and every few hours I'd make another sale. They trickled in, but there *was* a trickle and it was a money trickle. Emily and I were beside ourselves with excitement.

It struck me how writing an entire ebook to earn 300 measly dollars was something I was obsessively passionate about. I loved figuring out the technical hurdles on the computer to make the item for sale, writing the book, finding ways to creatively market the book—everything about it. Yet I earned much more than $300 by working at the dollar store and that was complete drudgery to me.

I've often been asked how I built a small business while being a full-time law student, being an intern, and working a part-time job. It really had nothing to do with self-discipline and certainly nothing to do with my time management skills, which were . . . um . . . not managed. The truth was that nothing could keep me from building the business. I had stumbled onto work that so perfectly matched my work energy I could not force myself to stop working on it.

> *Your work energy is so attractive to your mind that once you learn to turn it on, it will take all your willpower to turn it off.*

You have felt your work energy before. You've woken up early, excited to get going on a project. You've stayed up late working on something. You've had days where you loved working on something so much that you didn't notice the time. You likely didn't realize it wasn't the topic of what you were doing that fascinated you; it was the nature of the work. It wasn't your love for interior decorating that kept you from going to sleep until 2 a.m. so you could decorate the living room. It may have been your desire to please others, or the creative freedom involved. It was the nature of the work, not the topic of interior design. The same is true of every work energy. It is your mind's mechanism for achieving things according to the unique way you see them; it is the way you can best achieve greatness in the eyes of others.

My work energy was being fed as I watched the orange dots on the map pop up every time someone visited my site from a new location around the world. I was fascinated by the technology that made it possible to teach thousands of people at once. I fell in love with the thrill of thinking of a clever idea, implementing it on my site, and seeing that idea turn into revenue.

True Confession: My Work Energy

I had found my work energy. It wasn't photography that made me love working on my site. That just happened to be *the topic* of my site. My work energy was seeing that the world accepted me when I accomplished something difficult, like writing a book in two weeks or creating an online photography empire.

In short, my work energy is taking on tough challenges so others will be proud of me. Deep down inside, I think I need praise. There's a childish part of me that drives me to accomplish things that seem difficult to others. If my work energy could speak, it would say, "Look Ma! I'm amazing! Look at me! Nobody else can do *this*!"

And yes, it *is* embarrassing to write a book about work energy and then be forced to explain to everyone who reads this book that my personal work energy is that of a petulant child. Thank you for asking. It may be childish, but that's my work energy and it knows how to get things done in my mind. "Look Ma! I wrote a book! I bet Johnny can't do that!" Ugh.

My juvenile work energy is my own. Every individual's work energy is unique to them and likely comes from the individual life experiences in their past. Each person's mind finds its own drive to accomplish, and if you can identify it, you can turn it on any time you need it.

> *Once you identify your work energy,*
> *you can turn it on any time you need it.*

You know you have a work energy. If you have ever, even once, lost track of time when working on something or felt driven to wake up early, then you have a work energy. It has been there all along, and it's about to get things done for you.

About the same time I discovered my work energy, I had a conversation with a long-time friend. He told me about his job in technical support and how much he enjoyed it. I remember him saying something like, "Oh, I love my work! I'm getting paid to literally do almost nothing! It's so easy! All I have to do is sit at a desk and answer the phone or talk with people when they come into the office. They almost all have the same few issues, so I look like a rock star every time because I've fixed their same issue dozens of times each week for the last two years. It's the best job ever!"

I understood the words he said, but I couldn't fathom how he felt that way. From his description of his job, I would rather be waterboarded while receiving a root canal than have that job. I would rather watch baseball than have his job! There was no challenge. The tech support questions he answered were repetitive and dealt with only the basic part of his technical knowledge.

My work energy drives me to accomplish measurable goals that I perceive others couldn't achieve so I might receive praise from others. My friend's work energy is feeling useful by being able to confidently solve others' problems for them without ever being faced by a problem that would make him look unknowledgeable. His barricade is being in a situation where he is unsure of how to proceed. His work matched his work energy and avoided his barricade, so he was successful. If I worked in the same I.T. department, I would need to take on very different tasks to be happy and effective.

It was interesting to me that the topic of my work made no difference to my work energy. While I did enjoy photography, the topic of my website, I also enjoyed camping and technology and religion and politics and a lot of other things. There may have been some topics that would have been less fun to work on, but it wasn't the topic of the site that captivated me, it was the nature of the work. I could look at a suite of numbers like pageviews on the site, revenue, the average amount of time users stayed on the page, etc. With all those numbers to compete against each day, it was work heaven for me. My work energy was having concrete problems with no readily apparent solution, which I could improve with creativity.

When I was working at the dollar store, I saw difficult problems that I wanted to tackle to receive praise and acceptance. The delivery trucks usually came on Tuesdays, and a large crew was needed to unload the trucks. But those trucks were often late. The store paid for 10 employees to sit around and do nothing for up to an hour until the truck came. The store dealt with this problem by requiring us to be at work at a certain time but not allowing us to punch our time cards yet. We had to be there for an hour, unpaid, waiting for the delivery truck. Frankly, I think this was unethical if not illegal, and the employees were extremely unhappy about it.

I had solutions to that problem. Each week, they could simply leave one pallet of merchandise in the large back storeroom. We wouldn't stock those items onto the shelves until the delivery day the next week, so we'd have something to work on while waiting for the truck. It was a simple solution to a difficult problem that could have dramatically improved employee happiness, yet my manager could not have been less interested in hearing my suggestion. I was not empowered to use my work energy. The problem was not the company I worked for or the fact that it was a dollar store, it was that the type of work I was given did not match my work energy.

I got that wrong when I was in college. Most college students pick their career based on the topic of the work, and not the nature of the work. It leads most of us into careers that don't match our work energy. For example: A student has a biology teacher in high school who made the class enjoyable, so she goes into chemistry, which eventually leads her to medical school. In med school, she's mentored by a helpful pediatrician and selects that specialty because she enjoys learning about the topic.

Then she gets a full-time job and all of a sudden realizes that she hates the nature of the work. Angry, upset, grumpy patients come in every day. She spends five minutes with each one and treats the cold or flu so many times that at some point, it takes no real skill. There's nothing new in chemistry she's learning, and she finds that the hours of a pediatrician don't at all match the kind of lifestyle she wanted. She looks up, 15 years into her career, and is yearning for something else, wondering what's wrong with her and why she can't get her drive to achieve built back up. She picked chemistry because of the topic, but she should have instead focused on the *nature* of the work that would match what drives her and picked a career based on that drive—her work energy.

Suppose instead this same student spent some time paying attention to what drives her: her work energy. Is she happiest doing work when she is in motion all the time, like my wife; when she gets to share knowledge, like my business partner; when she gets to compete, like me? What is it that drives her? Then she could select a career or a job position that matches that drive—her work energy.

So what now? What do you do when you're 15 years into your career, wondering what got you there? Go back to college to pick a new major? Not likely. What if our fictional pediatrician really looked at herself and found what drives her energy, and then refocused her work to match that work energy? For example, if I were in that position, I may find a very enjoyable career as a healthcare administrator. I would love the job of looking at a budget and figuring out how we could see twice the number of patients without spending another dime on personnel. Or, as a traditional pediatrician, I may find more joy in my work by opening my own practice and working to increase revenue or other metrics I could compete against.

My work energy is achieving measurable things that I perceive others can't or won't, so I can get the approval of others. It's what drives me. Repetition shuts me down because I would have to do things I already know how to achieve or that I perceive as being so easy nobody will praise me for doing them. My friend in tech support has a different work energy: service. He feels most fulfilled when he can confidently fix things for people, while giant obstacles shut him down.

When I began to recognize how distinct each person's work energy is, I was amazed to understand so much of my life and the things that I had struggled with, all because of my own unique work energy. When I go out in the backyard to play catch with my boys, I can't last three minutes of simply throwing the ball back and forth without turning it into a competition. "Let's see how many in a row we can do without dropping it!" "Let's take a step back after each throw and see how far we can get!"

Learning my work energy helped me to understand how to be a better dad to my kids. I suddenly understood why, after planning and saving up for a vacation to go with my family to an amusement park, I felt so incredibly disengaged and dull walking around the park with them for a day. It made me feel guilty. "Do I not care about my kids enough? Why am I not enjoying this?" Then I understood my work energy and it changed how I spend time with them. I went on hard hikes with them, took them hunting, made a YouTube channel with them, and more. Those activities gave me an obstacle to overcome with them and I absolutely loved every minute I spent with them. If you love your kids but wonder why it's so exhausting to do things with them that should be enjoyable, the answer is that you aren't satisfying your work energy. And it's eating at you.

When my family goes on vacation, my first question is which new country I can go to. We've had many excellent vacations around the world, but I have a difficult time going to the same place twice because I need to check off a new country from my list. I need to be somewhere completely foreign to me, where it'll be hard to figure out travel and communicate with people in different languages. I'll never forget having a soldier with a massive rifle pointed at us when we tried to walk into a pyramid that was apparently off-limits in Egypt, or acting like a monkey on the sidewalk in Japan as I tried communicate to the taxi driver, who didn't speak English, that we wanted him to take us into the mountains where we could see the monkeys. If there's something hard to overcome, I'm in. This simple change to how I spend time with my kids has made me love being a dad.

At work, I am invigorated by numbers. When the outcome of my work can be measured by a simple metric, I am absolutely driven to make the number increase. As an online influencer today, I always have a metric I'm focused on. Pageviews to a website, views of a YouTube channel, podcast downloads, income from a product launch, number of articles written during a month, etc. I don't really care *what* I do. I don't care if I'm recording a podcast or making a YouTube video or writing an article on a particular day. The *type* of work matters little to me, as long as the work can be measured. I guess deep down inside I want to impress someone— maybe myself—and I feel I can best do that when there's a competition that can be measured.

Does that seem a little extreme? If so, it's likely because you have your own work energy, and you may not even realize it.

I have a friend who has a very distinct work energy, and when I recognized it, it helped endear her to me and appreciate her quirks.

She has three wonderful adopted children, a stalwart husband, and a great family. Yet she turns everyday events into insane situations. She sees the sky is falling at every moment, and you can see a little glimmer in her eye every time something goes wrong. She's constantly saying how crazy her children are, even when I see them as extremely obedient and kind. In short, she is all drama all the time, but in a fun way so you can tell she loves the insanity of it all. You cannot calm this woman down.

I would characterize her work energy as survivorship. Growing up rejected by her birth parents and in a chaotic situation, she had to learn to survive. That work energy drove her decision to become a social worker, prepared her for years of struggles in raising three children who were all adopted from drug-addicted parents, enabled her to help her husband who is also from a broken home, and gave her the strength to live through the loss of her mother. Because of what she has lived through, she has developed a work energy that allows her to thrive in difficult situations. She swims best in deep water. She thrives on difficulty because she wants to show others what she can overcome. Without realizing it, she even makes things in her life seem harder than they really are because she needs something to fight against. She's a fighter and feels her greatest fulfillment when she can flex that muscle of surviving difficult life situations.

My wife's work energy is motion. She needs to feel busy in order to feel happy with her daily work. Each morning we wake up at 5 a.m. to exercise, read scriptures, spend an hour together, and get ready for the day before the kids wake up. During that hour together, she rarely sits and talks to me. This morning, she folded laundry and assembled shelves while I sat on the couch talking with her. She doesn't need me to be in constant motion, but she needs to be. She really enjoys our time together but prefers to enjoy it on the move. She can't sit down to talk or she wouldn't enjoy it as much. Motion is what drives her and makes her feel happy. She applies her work energy to everything she does—even when that work isn't career-focused. Her work energy drives her to be the best stay-at-home mom, best Shaun T exercise nut, the best piano player, and the best person she can be.

My good friend and business partner, Ricky Kesler, has a work energy of sharing knowledge. Ricky was crazy good at school. In high school, he aced everything, every time. I was the B student, and he was the A++ student. By the way, the thing that annoys me most is how people get a GPA above 4.0. How is that even possible? Nerds. I hate nerds. I swear they go to these "National Honor Society" meetings to scheme about how they are going to convince the fools that it's possible to get more than 100% on a test and score more than a 4.0 GPA, and then snicker to themselves when they give a nonsense argument for it that the rest of us can't follow.

Anyway, when we're in business meetings, I don't bother with a calculator because I can just ask him and he'll immediately know the answer to complex math questions. I've never seen anything like it. However, school ended. Ricky completed high school, a bachelor's degree, and an MBA. Suddenly there were no more tests to work off his work energy, and no teachers to give him satisfying above-4.0 numbers just to spite all the dumb kids who couldn't even understand how that was possible.

Consequently, Ricky is happiest at work when he can share his knowledge. He doesn't particularly enjoy a brand-new project like I do because he doesn't feel he has unique knowledge to share. He has a difficult time on camera when he needs to ad-lib an explanation of something for a YouTube video, but when he teaches a class on something he knows about, he is absolutely in his element. Right now, at this very moment as I write this section of the book, we're at an industry conference called FinCon where we're speaking. One of the attendees booked a 15-minute session with him to ask him some questions. I found a very comfy chair to sit down and write this because I absolutely know he'll go very long with that appointment. When someone is asking him questions about a topic he knows well, he will go on forever. Why? Because he gets to flex his work energy. He thrives on doing Q&A webinars or Q&A presentations, because people come to him for his knowledge and he has a chance to share it. Update: That 15-minute appointment? It lasted 57 minutes. And yes, I clocked it.

Ricky gets bored with big-picture business meetings discussing marketing ideas. He can't show to others that he has the knowledge to a specific question when speaking creatively. In fact, he interrupts nearly every big-picture meeting with something like, "Hey! We just got an email from a customer who . . . " and then he tells us how the customer could fix the problem. We have a customer service specialist who handles those emails. That customer service specialist reports to our customer success director. There are two levels of people who should handle that email before Ricky, but he can't stop sharing his gift in that way. He is driven by sharing knowledge. It makes him a talented teacher and mentor, and it keeps our company focused on the individual customers who keep us in business. He—like all of us—has to feed his work energy to enjoy his workday.

Watching Ricky with his kids proves out his work energy even more. He is intensely focused on their academic performance and learning. His work energy dictates how he enjoys spending time with his family.

It may take you some time to discover your work energy and, depending on how well you know yourself and how many different types of work you've experienced, to understand what you enjoy and what you don't.

Here's an example for you. We have a marketing manager in our company named Freddy, and I sat down with him while writing this book to get a sense of his work energy. As we made our way through the action step for this chapter and Freddy told me about his past jobs, his family life, and his personal experiences, he came to realize his work energy wasn't what he previously thought. Turns out he's a people pleaser.

I don't mean that in the way you usually hear it, though. "People pleasers" are generally looked upon as disingenuous politicians, stealthily pushing their own agenda. Freddy just has an inherent need to give people what they want, for better or for worse. When he and his wife are making plans, he quietly tries to figure out what *she* is in the mood to do. Is it just because he is a kind and selfless husband? Heck no! He seeks approval from the world by giving others what they want. It is the mechanism his mind has developed for getting ahead. Another example is that his sense of humor tends to change drastically, depending on who he is with, for the same reason. He wants to see that those around him are satisfied. That's why he is perfect for marketing. He has an instinct that tells him what people want, and he knows how to tailor the narrative to them. He's living his work energy.

When you tap into your work energy, there won't be anything that can stop you from achieving, and I will help you discover yours. If you feel disengaged at work or feel that you have little willpower to stick to your goals, then you merely need to identify and learn to turn on the work energy that is currently lying dormant within you. High achievers are those who have developed their work energy into a weapon they can unleash on any goal they deem worthy of achieving, and soon you'll be among them.

When I began writing this book, several people encouraged me to develop a concept of three or four work energies so that people could more easily classify themselves. "You know, like the color personality test!" I simply haven't found that to be the case. Each person's drive is distinct, according to their specific talents and life experiences.

Your work energy usually develops from a desire to be viewed positively by others. I am the youngest of six high-achieving boys in my family and I wasn't particularly book smart in school, so I learned to compensate by achieving big goals to get noticed and coming up with creative ways of achieving them. My friend who was adopted wants others to see her as a survivor and be impressed with what she can live through. My friend Ricky wants others to see how smart he is. My wife was always the one people came to for help in her family when she was growing up, so now she loves being busy all the time in serving others.

What about you? What work energy has been driving your decisions and work all your life?

Action Step Two: Discover Your Unique Work Energy

What Drives You?

I warn you to not make snap judgments about your work energy. Not understanding yourself could lead you into a lifetime of picking the wrong types of work and wondering why you quickly become disinterested with them. Be open-minded in discussing this topic and remember you can always come back to these action steps by simply going to WorkEnergyBook.com/steps, so you don't have to stop reading right now.

The following seven questions have been carefully designed to help you discover your unique work energy. After you go through them for yourself, ask a spouse, family member or long-time friend to answer them about you. Another person may understand you better than you understand yourself.

1. What is your leadership and teaching style? If you have kids, you will identify this in your parenting. When you come up with something to play with your kids, what do you do? Do you find

yourself competing with them by timing them in races? Do you feel better when you're busy caring for necessities? Do you enjoy sitting on the sidelines watching them in sports games, or do you want to be the coach? What do you dream of your kids becoming? What unique family vacations would you like to take? Looking at your parenting approach is a clear insight into your work energy. If you don't have children, look at how you teach others or how you lead.

2. What unique life experiences forced you to learn certain traits? You'll enjoy doing work when you naturally feel strong and comfortable with the behaviors and attitudes required to do what's necessary. How did you overcome situations that made you sad and worried? How has your birth order in your family affected your personality? What did your parents teach you?

3. Who is someone you loved, but whose personality others found off-putting? What helped you to understand them?

4. What would a perfect workday look like at your current job? If you could design the nature of your work, what would that be?

5. What do you intentionally do to impress other people? What do you make a point of mentioning to make sure others see you in the way you want to be seen?

6. What character trait are you proud of in yourself?

7. When you were growing up, what was something hard to do that you enjoyed working on?

You may already have work that matches your work energy. If so, you need this book just as much as someone who is currently performing soul-grinding work because that's the only way you'll be able to turn on your work energy—when you know what it is.

This book isn't just about your career. It's about igniting a fire in your bones that drives you in every aspect of your life. How could you enjoy your kids more by matching your time with them to your work energy? How could you finally learn the guitar by setting up a training method that matches the way you like to work?

Another group of readers may not know what they want to pursue at all. If that's you, I encourage you to fill your mind with education. Subscribe to 20 podcasts and binge-listen. Expose your mind to a wide range of ideas, thoughts, hobbies, and interests. It likely won't be long before you find something that begins to kindle a little fire in your bones. When it does, consider your work energy and how you could apply it to that endeavor.

You don't need to know all the answers right now. As we pursue this concept throughout the book, you'll read dozens of examples of those who have successfully identified the work that matches their work energy, and it will help you to identify your best work.

If you find yourself stuck in your career and wondering where your passion went, stop focusing on the industry you're in or the topic of your work. Focus on what *type* of work drives you. Focus on what your work energy is, and how you could adjust your thinking or position within that industry to better match it.

Fail to understand your work energy, and you may never ignite the fire in your bones. Your work energy, the thing that drives you, is within you. What is it?

3

SUMMON YOUR DREAMING JUICES

> *"I had a dream once."*
> *—The big dude in the tavern in the Disney movie*
> *Tangled that my daughter has watched so many*
> *times I can't think of any other quote without first*
> *thinking of that guy. So let's all just pretend it's a*
> *meaningful quote and move on.*

After the initial sale of my ebook and shamelessly plugging it while posing as a caller to Leo Laporte's radio show, I was hooked. I only earned $300 and sales quickly slowed to a trickle, but it was a trickle nonetheless.

I wish I could adequately express how I felt. The freaking internet sent me a check! It felt unreal. People I'd never met were sending money to my PayPal account and I didn't have to do any additional work for a sale.

I set my sights. I'd had my back against the wall financially for too long, and I finally saw a path forward. I was going to make an online business and nothing could stop me.

Usually, our biggest dreams in life are simply ways to compensate for a past perceived failure. I failed my family financially and now I knew how I'd compensate for it, going forward. I only had to figure out how to make this goal a reality.

Sales mostly ran dry after a week. It turned into just a random drop. Every two or three days, someone would come to the website and pick up the

$5 ebook. I checked my online dashboard every few days and was disappointed to see no sales coming in at all.

I immediately began working on my second book and continued writing on the site as I feigned attention in my classes.

"Mr. Harmer, a schoolboy kicked another boy and then the injured boy got a freak infection in his leg. Was the boy who kicked the other child liable for the infection?"

I felt like saying, "I have no idea, but the internet sent me a check!"

A few months later, I was up late watching orange dots appear on my website's map and writing a list of articles on the site. Emily was on the couch asleep beside me. I hadn't checked my ebook dashboard in a while, so I decided to see if I'd finally made a sale there yet. I was certain the new ebook craze on the iPad would have brought in sales, yet there had been absolutely zero activity on this dashboard for months.

When I logged in, I found an account payable balance of $1,935.27. I couldn't understand it. Had all that happened in one day? No—it looked like the sales were spread out over a few months, but I hadn't seen anything! I dug through the entire website and finally found it—sales were only reported quarterly. I was certain there was some kind of trick. That *couldn't* be real, but it was.

I kneeled down in front of Emily, woke her up, and said, "I think I just earned $2,000!" We spent at least two hours reading every word on the website to ensure we weren't getting ahead of ourselves. I had actually earned almost $2,000 from my little ebook project.

At least 100 more refreshes of my account dashboard later, a check was in the mail for my earnings, and I actually received it.

We needed the money desperately. Emily and I didn't even have a bed—just an old mattress on the floor in our apartment. We certainly had no money for decorations in our little apartment, so Emily bought some colorful circular placemats and tacked them on the walls. It looked about as good as you're imagining.

A dream began to grow within me. Although we needed the money, I began to dream of building my online presence into an actual business rather than just a one-off side hustle I'd done to earn a couple hundred dollars from an ebook. I dared to allow myself to see something much larger, and it allowed me to reinvest in a fledgling business.

> *I began to dream of building my online presence into an actual business rather than just a one-off side hustle.*

It was about this time that Nikon announced a revolutionary new camera—the Nikon D7000. I felt sick to my stomach about spending that much money on a camera, but Emily and I decided together that there was an opportunity with this website, so we'd reinvest every single dollar we'd earned. I bought a camera, a lens, and an inexpensive tripod.

We so badly needed the money that I'm amazed we didn't use it on a few necessities at home. A dream is a powerful thing, and if you will summon your dreaming juices and allow those dreams to grow, you may find yourself taking action on things you don't yet dare vocalize to others.

The Dream Catches Fire

The website grew slowly until my third year of law school, when it saw an explosion of traffic and earnings.

I continued putting out books. Two, three, four, five books—and all of them were selling. They generally got positive reviews, but they were also short and homemade.

At the same time, the traffic on the website continued to grow as I published articles almost every day on a wide variety of photography topics. In 2011, my traffic went from 23,000 pageviews per month to over 300,000 pageviews per month.

I had a straightforward approach to getting traffic to the website. I published new articles almost daily. Because I'd spent a year watching the orange dots, I got pretty good at guessing what topics for articles would get the most traffic.

On the podcasts I listened to, the hot new topic was online video courses, and I decided to sell one of my own. By this point, I had grown a significant following on Facebook. I used the 300,000 pageviews per month to push my website visitors over to Facebook to like our page. I had 50,000 Facebook followers at the time.

I was ready to take action on what I was learning because my work energy was being fed. I had become good at writing blog posts that drove traffic, and I needed a new challenge to conquer that was measurable so I could know people liked what I made. After some late-night strategy meetings with Emily, we decided to sell an online photography basics course for $75. The course would last 30 days, and I'd email my students a video lesson each day. Why didn't they get all 30 lessons at once? Because I hadn't created them yet. I made the video each day to send out that night. I wanted to do a good job for my customers and I did my best, but I was very much a new business owner making all kinds of mistakes.

I created a sales funnel introducing my Photography 101 course and then announced it on Facebook. I was really nervous, but also extremely excited to see if someone would spend that much money on a course with me.

I refreshed the page 60 seconds after making the post on Facebook, and the entire course was sold out. I had sold 50 seats in the course at $75 each, and it was sold out in one rotation of the second hand. I stared at a PayPal balance of $3,750.

I'm so sorry for whoever took my first online course. Looking back, it was an absolute train wreck. The lighting was awful, the photos I took were mediocre at best, and I looked scared to death in the video. Seriously, I'm sorry, but at the time I was really proud of my work as it was the best I could do.

The next month, I increased the number of seats in the class to 75 and raised the price to $99. It took two minutes and 20 seconds to sell out. I had earned $7,425 in two minutes. I was beside myself.

The next month, I really stretched myself and took on 100 students, who could email me questions or get feedback on their photos from me as often as they wanted during the 30-day class. Sure enough, it sold out in a matter of seconds. I earned almost $10,000 in less than a minute.

I was entirely overwhelmed at this point. Full-time law school, full-time internship at the Ada County Prosecutor's Office, and running a company that was becoming quite profitable. But I couldn't stop. The virtual praise I received by seeing the numbers of people coming to my website fed my work energy and drove me to accomplish bigger and bigger feats in the business.

After Emily and I had the horrible experience buying the scam car in Florida, the replacement for that car finally died out as well. We went to the car lot expecting to buy a used car, but we found a base model Nissan Sentra for $14,000 and we bought it brand-new.

In 2011, my blog earned $77,843—more than a lawyer's starting salary. I applied for a job as an attorney and was offered it. My salary upon graduating from law school would be about $60,000. I owed $90,000 in student loans. I would now have my income as an attorney, and the income from my website. That was exciting.

I transferred for my last year of law school to a school in Idaho, where I worked with low-income people with legal needs. I worked on a complicated case that was crushingly stressful for a young law student with many other things going on. My client was a widow in her 80s living in California. Her late husband was an investment advisor who had helped clients for years with their investments—even as dementia slowly overcame his mind. The inevitable errors in his work came to light only after his death, and his widow was swamped with lawsuits. It was my responsibility to untangle a decade-long rat's nest of error-ridden paperwork.

I felt pressured to get the project done, so I worked on it late every night, as winter and Christmas approached. I woke up early on Christmas Eve to return to the job. I arrived in the office before the light of day and got started.

A Christmas Eve Decision

Around noon, I walked out of the conference room to my cubicle and saw huge flakes of snow floating onto the downtown Boise landscape. In my mind, I could imagine the squeals of delight from my two little boys at home as they dreamed of their presents and candy and played from sunrise to sunset. Rather than feeling sad, something in me snapped. There were two boxes of papers between me and my family. Suddenly, I realized I was missing one of the most important moments of my life—Christmas Eve with my wife and two boys. From that instant on, I promised myself I was going to be in the driver's seat when it came to my career. There was no way I would allow work or poverty to control my family any longer.

I did what I was supposed to do. I got a bachelor's degree and where did it lead me? To the dollar store with no other job prospects. I went to law school and where did that lead me? To $90,000 in debt and unable to provide for the basic necessities for my family—alone in an empty office on Christmas Eve.

Until that day, I had viewed my blog as a tremendous second income. Christmas Eve changed that. Sure, I understood that the vast majority of attorneys were not working on Christmas Eve, but I didn't want to be in a situation again where work or finances controlled us. I was going to take complete control.

My work energy had driven me to this point in my business, and I was going to pursue it. I allowed myself to dream about what life could look like if I unleashed my work energy full time. The only problem? Somehow I had to break it to my wife, who had just spent three years caring for the kids single-handedly and sacrificing financially so I could get a law degree that I was now thinking about abandoning.

You have dreams too. There is something you want to achieve. It may be as simple as learning to juggle or as complicated as changing your work to best fit your work energy. It may be repairing your marriage or meeting a sales goal. There are things you want to accomplish, and I've learned that the mere act of acknowledging those dreams can give them the life they need to drive you to accomplish them.

For example, when I was 15 years old, I created a bucket list of 50 things to do in life. I created the list and mostly forgot about it for many years. I unearthed it in my old journals when I was in my 20s. I was shocked to see how many of the things on that list I had accomplished—some of them quite specific and difficult, such as singing a solo in front of 2,000 people or more and becoming a student body officer in college.

I had forgotten about the specific listed goals, but merely having that list had solidified in the back of my mind the things I would do and the kind of person I would become. Now, only a decade later, I have accomplished 35 of the things on the list. Sometimes I changed the original goals I made as a teenager, when they didn't reflect my current desires, but I've never nerfed any goals to make them easier. Here are a few highlights of goals that I've accomplished.

- See the northern lights
- Read a dictionary from cover to cover
- Buy a house with cash
- Run a full 26.2-mile marathon
- Coach little league football
- Write a book that sells 2,000 copies
- Save someone's life
- Be a millionaire
- Earn a doctorate-level degree
- Learn to speak a second language fluently

I was in law school earning a Juris Doctorate degree so I could mark off the doctorate-level degree. I had just written an ebook that sold over 2,000 copies. It was incredible how simply writing down that list and dreaming as a teenager effectively charted a course for my life without even realizing its effect. I had entirely forgotten about my bucket list, but because those goals had been dreamed somewhere in the back of my mind, I went after them as natural life opportunities arose. Goals are valuable, whether or not they are the type of goal you mark off days on a calendar to achieve.

Action Step Three: Summon Your Dreaming Juices

Now it's your turn to dream about what you would like to achieve and who you would like to be in the future. Think broadly about your life as a whole rather than narrowing your focus to one specific short-term goal.

Write Down Your Dream

Do not think of the steps you would have to take to accomplish them, or whether you think you can get them done. This isn't a to-do list. This is simply a dream. Be specific about your goals. Some of them can be stupid like reading a dictionary cover-to-cover, and others should shape who you become, like having a family.

So write it down. What would you like to achieve? Dream like a 15-year-old who has no concept of logistics. The question is not *how*, but *what*.

Some people struggle to dream because their minds immediately jump to the difficulties in achieving the goal and a determination of how practical the goal is. If this is you, I'll share one piece of advice from someone who has learned to dream big:

Let your dreams breathe for one minute.

Everyone is creative and wants to achieve things, but most people are too practical to allow those ideas to survive their scrutiny. Simply write down things you would like to be or do. Later you'll learn a framework to make the logistics the simplest part of the process.

What experiences like I had on Christmas Eve have you also had but haven't yet been able to realize? Retire early? Love your job again? Get promoted? Earn your bonus at the end of this year? Get married? Develop a relationship with God? Summon your dreaming juices.

You won't be asked to make a goal like we're all taught in school. It doesn't have to be specific, measurable, time bound, etc. It may be, but it doesn't have to be. Just like my bucket list with no end-date except the end of my life, some goals can be very effective without locking you into a specific schedule. Other goals, like achieving a sales target, do need specific requirements to hold your feet to the fire.

While most people can quickly identify things they have dreamed in their future, others struggle to have such a clear vision. If that is the case, I'd encourage you to make a full bucket list of 50 things to do in life. It has served me well in clarifying in my mind where I want to go. Look up others' bucket lists online and get inspired. Talk to your family and friends and ask them what they want to do. Dream a future.

Here's your chance to become something that you aren't today. Here's your chance to go somewhere or do something you've never done before. What is it?

.

4

GOING ROGUE AND BUYING BRICKS

> *"The only thing standing between you and everything you've ever wanted to do in life—is doing it."*
> *—Casey Neistat*

Once I dreamed the thought of running my business full-time, I couldn't put it away. And I needed to turn my attention to the logistics of *how* I would achieve it. What if, after all this hard work, sacrifice, and struggle—not to mention $90,000 in student loan debt—I didn't actually practice law? How could I tell my wife that?

I've never been able to keep anything from Emily. Even when I have a surprise for her, I end up spilling the beans every time. Two weeks before her birthday, we'll be driving down the road and "I got you a beautiful new bracelet!" will just pop out of my mouth. It's an illness. I guess there were those times when I told her we were going to a restaurant and the kids and I surprised her by taking her to the airport for a secret vacation, but that was only after many years of not being able to keep a thing from her. I'm better at keeping secrets from my wife now. Don't tell her.

Even when we were dating, I had the "spill everything to Emily" illness. We had only been on two dates before it hit me that I'd like to marry her someday. Any normal person would keep that to themselves for a long time, but precisely seven days after our first kiss, I proposed. Seven weeks later, we were married.

We have been through a lot together, but this was a bigger test for our marriage than we'd faced before. How do you wake up one morning, roll over to talk to your spouse, and say, "Uh . . . schmoopsie poo? Remember how we spent $90,000 on law school, and you scrimped and sacrificed, taking care of our two little babies full time and keeping the house while I basically lived at the law library on a ruined wingback blue chair over the last three years to become a lawyer? You remember that? And do you remember how we were going to have my income as an attorney *and* the income from my blog to support us to change all of that? Well, I was thinking about trading in my suit and tie for some sweats and a T-shirt so I can lounge around at home all day and blog from my laptop."

I don't know how that would go in most marriages, but here's how it went in mine. As soon as I said it, Emily responded, "I know it seems crazy, but I think you can do it, Jim! I've been wondering if you should go for it, and now that you're bringing it up too, I think that means you should."

All it took to begin the momentum toward my goal was taking that very first step of removing the distraction of my job as an attorney. I turned down the job I'd been offered and prepared to go a different direction. There would never be a salary or pension in my future, or a boss to simply tell me what to do each day. We were going rogue. We decided to take the future into our own hands and see how far we could take the opportunity.

There's something you want to accomplish, too. Otherwise, you wouldn't have bought this book. Would you like to have boundless energy to spend every day teaching your kids as a stay-at-home mom? What country do you want to travel to? What social issue would you love to work on? Would you like to do something in politics? Write a book? Climb a mountain? Run a marathon? Learn Spanish? Every person alive has something in their mind they'd like to do or accomplish.

I learned *how* you can accomplish those goals in Brazil.

I lived in Brazil for two years as a missionary. One day, I went to visit a man named Marcos in a rural community outside Itù. My companion and I had been to his house a number of times, and I noticed a small stack of 15-20 bricks behind Marcos's house. The next time we visited, I noticed the bricks were arranged differently and there were a few more. Again, on a third visit, I thought the stack seemed slightly larger. Eventually, I asked him jokingly if he was starting a collection.

He answered, "Someday, we will have children, and I'm going to have enough bricks to make a room for them."

I asked him when he was going to pick up the rest of the bricks and he responded, "I don't really know when I'll have enough bricks. Every time I have a little extra money, I buy a few more bricks and carry them home." That attitude taught me something about achieving big goals:

All big goals are achieved by small starting steps.

Contrast Marcos's attitude to a painter I met not long ago. He was lamenting to me that he was having a difficult time finding enough jobs painting houses. His business wasn't doing well, and it was stressful for him. He even said he wasn't sure if painting houses was the future he'd like to have. Remembering the hidden blessing I found while working at the dollar store of being able to listen to podcasts, I suggested that the painter use his many quiet work hours to learn skills that could improve his situation. He could not have been less interested in my suggestion. He just looked at me with an expression of someone who had just watched Star Trek and baseball for a few hours.

I wish I could personally sit down with you and talk about your bucket list, and how you could accomplish it. I wish I could work on them with you and bust them out together. I wish I could come to your house and sit in your living room and drink a root beer with you, but that would be strange. I digress.

Let's keep this simple. Imagine I'm sitting in front of you, talking with you face to face. You tell me the goal you've dreamed, and I tell you this: "Prove it. You want it so bad? I dare you to just take one step."

People can dream all they want, but the vast majority of people will dream the rest of their lives away. Do you have a goal and you really mean it? I dare you to actually do one tiny thing about it today.

Want a bigger house? Go spend $5 on a brick.

Want to lose weight? I dare you to eat only a small salad for dinner tonight. Just tonight. One time.

Want to be a better dad? I dare you to take your kid camping this weekend, even if you've never done it before.

Want to get a college degree? I dare you to request your high school transcript.

Want to go to New Zealand? I dare you to sell something from your garage on Craigslist and put the money in your savings account.

You won't, though. At least, statistically, you won't. According to the University of Scranton, 81% of people are unable to maintain their New Year's resolution goals long term (Vangarelli and Norcross, "The resolution solution: longitudinal examination of New Year's change attempts.").[2]

Very few people actually do anything about their goals. We just like to dream of a time when we might achieve in the future, and regret that we didn't achieve in the past. If you don't harness your work energy, you'll be a lazy lump of lard who won't achieve your goal because it's "too hard."

Yes, I'm trying to provoke you. No, I don't actually know if you are in fact a lazy lump of lard. I want to poke the bear. If you care at all about bettering your situation, I dare you to take the tiniest, simplest, easiest step toward your goal today.

Three years ago, I told my wife I wanted to learn the guitar. One of the things on my bucket list is to play "Time of Your Life" on the guitar. Why did I pick the most cliché song ever to learn on the guitar? Because I'm a cliché kind of guy, okay? Give me some slack. My wife researched and researched and bought me a beautiful guitar. On Christmas morning, I excitedly opened the gift wrapped in the peculiar shape of a guitar case. I was thrilled to see the tool I'd use to knock another item off my list. I tuned it up and printed off the chords to "Time of Your Life" by Green Day as well as fingering diagrams for each of the most common chords. That guitar case has not been opened a single time in the ensuing three years. I kid you not. I can be a lazy lump of lard too, if I don't intentionally fight against it.

So when I say you're a lazy lump of lard, I'm not throwing stones. I'm calling you a human being, and human beings are simply not good at daring to take the first step toward dreams. We almost always lean toward the comfort of doing what we have always done.

Here's why I feel so adamantly that you must take some kind of step today before you go to sleep. I'll explain it with a story.

A few years ago, a friend of mine came to my house and asked for help. He was struggling financially and wanted to learn how to create an income online. I had the perfect opportunity for him. I owned a website about baseball that I had purchased as an investment. The site had decent traffic already. As you've gathered from my writings thus far, I do not like baseball. This friend loved it. I offered that he could write blog posts about baseball on the site and better monetize the solid traffic the site was getting. I'd give him everything the site earned after the amount it was already earning. It was an incredible opportunity for him. I had a site with a great start and decent traffic, it was on a topic he was familiar with, and I'd be mentoring him through every step of the process. I spent several hours showing him exactly what he needed to do, and he left my house extremely excited to get going and for what this opportunity meant for him.

Two years later, I logged back into the baseball site. Guess what? He never once wrote a single article, never touched the site, never made any improvements, and the site had died out.

Humans are experts at freezing up and choking at the moment when we need to swing for the fences. We all do it.

That wasn't the only time this had happened. After I successfully built my business, I had over a dozen friends and family members come to my kitchen table and pour their hearts out about how desperately they wanted to start an online business making content. Each time they left with a clear tutorial on what to do and my offer to spend as much time with them as they needed. Seriously, this happened at least a dozen times or more. Each time they'd assure me they'd be the exception who would immediately get to work on the opportunity. There were a few who did and fizzled out in a month or less, but most of them never even took step one.

I should add at this point that I am also a lazy lump of lard. Yes, I took the opportunity to start a business, but do you know how many times I've been "sooo incredibly committed to start a diet today!"? It's embarrassing. Trust me, I'm a lazy lump of lard just like you are. Given the right circumstances, we're all lards. Boy, I hope that the last sentence isn't the one line from this book that gets quoted in reviews.

Action Step Four: Take One Step Toward the Goal You Want

Few readers of this book will suddenly shift careers or suddenly quit their job to blog in their pajamas. Please don't do that. It sounds like a terrible idea.

Yet every reader can buy a brick today, so to speak. Update your resume for your dream job that matches your work energy and just stick it on Monster.com. What do you have to lose? Open a note on your iPhone and write a plan for losing weight that matches your work energy. Go out and play with your kids by doing something you'd really enjoy, rather than being a martyr and following your kids around the local trampoline park like a zombie.

Want to travel the world but have no money? Go put $5 in your savings account right this second. Want to start an online business? Go buy your .com right now and tell yourself that someday you're going to write on it.

It doesn't matter how desperate you feel you are, or how badly you want to achieve your goal. It doesn't matter how resolute you feel now or how big you dream. The truth is you're about to choke big time. Yes, I'm provoking you again. I dare you to just take one step forward toward your goal and prove to me that you're the exception. Do it today. Something concrete, something today. Go buy your brick.

Just go buy a single brick. It doesn't matter if you don't have the blueprints for the whole house yet. You're going to need a brick, so every brick is one brick closer.

And if you don't buy the brick, you might be a lump of lard—but keep coming back to your goal and try again. Keep thinking about it and dream about how your life could change. What do you have to lose? A brick?

5

GROUNDHOGGING SUCCESS

> *"When Chekhov saw the long winter, he saw a winter*
> *bleak and dark and bereft of hope. Yet we know that*
> *winter is just another step in the cycle of life. But*
> *standing here among the people of Punxsutawney*
> *and basking in the warmth of their hearths and*
> *hearts, I couldn't imagine a better fate than*
> *a long and lustrous winter."*
> *—Bill Murray in* Groundhog Day

I had a clear goal to reach financial security for my family by building my online business full time, and I'd taken the first initial step by turning down a job as an attorney so I could focus on that goal. Now the work of growing and scaling that business was in front of me.

One of the first things I did was to hire an employee. I had started to become addicted to business books and podcasts, and I kept hearing that if I wanted to build a "real" company, I needed to "work on the business and not in the business." I read the book *The E-Myth*[3] and was putting it into practice religiously.

I went back to my alma mater—Brigham Young University-Idaho—and asked a well-respected professor for some advice on who I might find to help me with my website business. I hired a guy named Dustin almost on the spot because, frankly, I didn't know who else I'd get.

Dustin helped to manage the students in the online photography course so I could be sure their needs were being met. He was a diligent worker and someone I could generally rely on.

I graduated from law school in the spring and invited Dustin to come on full time when he finished school. It was a real company, and the revenue continued its ascent month after month.

I began looking for office space to run the company—because a real company needs a real office, I reasoned. I wanted somewhere that could function as both a full-fledged photography studio with high ceilings and an office. This way we could do video tutorials in our studio space and computer work in our computer space.

The building I rented was on historic Main Street in the little town of Caldwell, Idaho. The former bank building was over 100 years old. There are still four working vaults there with giant, two-foot-thick metal doors, which really gave the place character. I loved the old downtown location and the uniqueness of the building. I remember the meter reader coming over to turn on the power. It took him several hours to figure out which meter ran to our building because of the complicated nest of old wiring.

As we continued building traffic on the website by writing articles and sharing things on Pinterest, the revenue continued to climb. Eventually, we started hitting $20,000 per month reliably, and sometimes far exceeded it. The expenses of the business were actually quite low with only one employee and an inexpensive old building, so we were beginning to bring in a handsome profit.

A few weeks into this new venture and after graduating from law school, I decided it was time to create a podcast of my own. For some reason, I got it into my head that the bank vault would be the coolest possible spot to record a podcast from, so I went to the nearest hardware store and bought $200 worth of thick foam pads to quiet the echo from the metal walls. The show launched to great success with over 20,000 downloads in just the first week.

Emily and I bought our first house around this time. It was a basic 1,984 square-foot home because the builder knew it would annoy me that they hadn't added in an extra 16 square feet. The home was in the most inexpensive area of Caldwell, Idaho—a suburb of Boise. With the housing market in shambles, we were able to scoop up the house for $84,000 and we paid cash. It was hard to believe—we were not only first-time homeowners, but we owned our home outright. I nearly lost my mind when I sat down at a conference room table in the title company's office and wrote out a check for $84,000. I never thought I'd write a check that large in my entire life. Incidentally, that same home today is worth over $250,000.

Dave Ramsey is right about one thing. When you own a home outright, the carpet feels better, the grass feels thicker, and the whole thing is wonderful. We owned our own home without a mortgage, and it felt incredible, especially because of where we had come from.

I began tracking my net worth on a simple Excel sheet around this time. In September 2013, I had $90,000 of student loan debt. That number felt impossible to overcome. After I typed in all the numbers in my Excel sheet, I had a pit in my stomach thinking about the magnitude of the amount—$90,000. I would be paying for the degree that was collecting dust in a frame on my wall for the next decade. I was in financial prison: $90,000.

After the initial shock wore off, I made a simple plan. We had been broke before. In fact, we had been the *other* kind of broke before. We would simply reduce our expenses to that level, and I would write a blog post every single day on my website to increase traffic and help on the income side. My Excel sheet reported that at my current pace, this would be a years-long process.

As it would turn out, I was able to pay off the entire amount just 174 days later. Yes, we saved a significant amount of money by living frugally, but also my simple practice of writing a blog post a day had been the perfect fuel for my business. It had quickly boomed to bring in more income.

As the leaves began to fall off the trees, the romantic old bank-building-turned-podcasting-studio had over a dozen uninsulated gigantic glass windows along its front. Speaking of insulation, there didn't seem to be any in the walls either.

We kept the heat pumping 24/7 on full blast, but it only got colder in the building. I got called over during the middle of a date with Emily one night because the pipes had frozen upstairs and were leaking down into our portion of the building. Fortunately, nothing was ruined. The restaurant owner upstairs apologized, and we became friendly acquaintances. I loved the small-town feel of my little office.

Yet it continued getting colder. With the heat on full blast, we came into the office one morning and could see our breath. I got a thermometer which read 35 degrees—inside the office. We literally wore coats and gloves all day until Dustin made an offhand remark about what OSHA would think of these working conditions.

It was time to leave the bank and the bank-vault-turned-podcasting-studio.

We found another office space and after a few annoying days of moving furniture and equipment, we were all settled in the new spot. This was an old building, but it didn't have any character—orange carpet, drop ceiling, musty smell. I've always been a bit of a cheapskate.

I got a call one day from the guy who rented the restaurant above our old office space. As soon as I realized who was on the phone, I was surprised by the shake in his voice. I could tell that he was terrified to be calling me. I said, "Hey Mike, what's up? You sound upset."

He said, "Look, I'm a Christian and I've always tried to be an honest person, but the truth is gonna cost me my business today. Have you noticed how expensive your utility bills were in your office over here?"

I said that I had noticed and that it was because there was no insulation—that's why we moved out.

He replied, "Well, there's another reason. The meter reader messed up our lines and it turns out that you were paying for not only your space but also my space. Restaurants have huge energy bills—especially with this old equipment we have. Anyway, I was able to figure out how much I owe you and it's several thousand dollars. The problem is that the restaurant is just barely scraping by. After paying everybody, there's nothing left at the end of the month. So I'm calling to tell you that I can't pay you today, but I will sell off whatever equipment I need to and pay you back as soon as possible."

That's the kind of man we need in this world. I was surprised by his honesty and of course, wanted to help him out, so I told him I would just consider it a sunk cost and not worry about paying me. I realized for the first time that having money was a fantastic tool to do good.

I could have *wanted* to help him out if I were poor, but most people simply aren't in a position where they can reasonably forgive thousands of dollars of debt just to be nice. I saw that having money allowed me to do things I simply couldn't do before.

I'll always remember how cool it was to be able to help the restaurant owner in a time of need, and the only reason I got that chance was because I dreamed a goal to get out of debt, and I took daily actions to get there. Following your dreams opens up all kinds of doors.

It was still the early days of my business, and my simple daily efforts brought quick growth. Working on anything is fun during the rapid growth stage. After the work has been identified, the difficult starting period overcome, and the wheels are in motion, the work is exciting as you watch how far the initial steps propel you.

If you dream of being skinny, losing the first five pounds takes incredible self-discipline and faith that your hard work will bring about the desired result. After the first five pounds, the excitement of the rapid progress builds and it becomes easier to continue.

Learning a language is drudgery when you have to memorize the first 300 words and learn the conjugations. Then, once you can hold a basic conversation in the language, the remainder of learning becomes fun as you see the progress of your efforts.

The rapid progress stage of working toward any goal most often occurs when the learner understands the one thing they do that brings about 90% of the results. For me, I found that the time writing new blog posts and creating podcasts was bringing 90% of the success. More people came to the site, and thus I had more opportunities to make money. There were countless other things I could do such as improving the design of the site, creating more digital products, keeping up on the accounting, optimizing my site's speed, and taking pictures myself to improve my skills. Yet I was able to identify the single action that brought the vast majority of the success. If I published some piece of new content each day, the business continued to grow even if all of the other aspects of the business were imperfect.

Someone losing weight may find that focusing on simply eating fewer calories is far more important than a more optimized exercise routine. Someone wanting to retire may find that getting rid of a car payment is far more important than canceling Netflix. Someone wanting to be a better parent can simply set aside 30 minutes each day to get down on the floor and play with their kids rather than taking a parenting class, reading parenting blog posts on Pinterest, or spending more time at work to earn money for a big family vacation.

Design Your Day to Produce 90% of the Results

After building my first online business, in the ensuing decade I've built a dozen sites from the ground up to success. I was recently asked how I've built so many web businesses. Millions of people try to build blogs and YouTube channels without reaching success, but I've done it a dozen times or more. I had to think about it for a moment, but I realized that I always do the same thing. I identify the one thing that needs to be done in the business to drive 90% of the results. Then, I design a day where I can accomplish that one high-value activity, and I simply repeat that day like it's Groundhog Day.

Remember the movie *Groundhog Day?* In the 1993 movie with Bill Murray and Andie McDowell, the main character was stuck in a loop. He would live out one day, which happened to be Groundhog Day, and the next day he'd wake up the morning of Groundhog Day again.

Here's an example of how groundhogging a goal can work. When I was in college and realized I wanted to go to law school, I knew it would be expensive and the best way for me to avoid that expense would be a scholarship. I also knew that I had a below-average 2.8 GPA, and I frankly wasn't the best guy out there when it came to taking standardized tests. Worse yet, most law school hopefuls were paying thousands of dollars for a complete course on how to do well on the Law School Admissions Test (LSAT). I didn't have that kind of money.

Yet I managed to get an almost full-tuition scholarship to law school, which saved me a massive amount of money. Here's how I did it.

First, I knew that I thrived on achieving difficult tasks where I could measure my progress. "Look Ma! I got a good grade on the test!" That's my work energy. Eighteen months before I took the LSAT, I bought every single previous test of the LSAT that had ever been given. After a test is used, they publish the previous version so students can use it as a pre-test. I also spent about $50 on used versions of some of the old test prep books on eBay.

Then, I designed a day that would eventually make me a master at the LSAT. It was simple. Each morning, I'd wake up and spend 15 minutes researching law schools to determine where I wanted to go and what it'd take to get there. I needed to increase my GPA, so I simply made one change to my schedule—I spread out my classes so I'd have an hour after each class to study what had been taught or to do my homework. As soon as I got home from school but before I could be done for the day, I'd sit down for 30 minutes to study LSAT tips from the old books from eBay. Then every Wednesday, I'd take a full test, which lasted about three and a half hours. I planned for that time by not taking any classes on Wednesday afternoons. I created a graph on a piece of paper where I'd track my test score each Wednesday so I could compete with myself to maximize my work energy.

The day I "groundhogged" was designed to focus on only the most essential things I could do to move toward the goal. Rather than optimizing my note-taking in class, for example, I simply set up my day to ensure I did my homework. Ask any straight-A student and they'll tell you that the most important thing you can do to be a better student is never get a zero on an assignment to drag down your grade.

I started the very next day, and then just groundhogged it, living the same schedule each day until the LSAT. I wasn't a genius, and in fact, I had proven to be a below-average student, but I groundhogged the actions that gave me 90% of the result and I ignored every other optimization.

The night before the test, I had to drive to a city a few hours away. I went to sleep early so I'd feel my best for the test, but it did little good. I was so nervous that I woke up at 3 a.m. and stared at the ceiling for a while before getting up to look over my books and read through all the questions I had missed on the practice tests over the last year.

I arrived at the testing center early and heard all of the other students greeting each other who had been in test-prep classes together. I had focused on the most high-value activities, but I wondered if it would be enough compared to all of the other students.

The test was strictly timed, and I felt I was falling behind. I could figure out all of the problems easily if I had enough time, but the LSAT forces test-takers to understand logic quickly. After the test was over, I wasn't sure how I'd performed, but it was done. All I could do was wait.

I wasn't sure what to do with myself in the weeks after the test. I had established such a strict schedule to groundhog for the previous year that it was hard not to be studying anymore.

Finally, my test score arrived. I opened up the letter and timidly looked at my score. I was in the 85th percentile of all test takers, and it would likely be good enough to get a scholarship. Because of the 15 minutes I'd spent each morning researching law schools, I knew precisely what schools I'd apply to, and it wasn't long before acceptance letters started arriving (and a few denials).

The result came because I identified a way that I could prepare for the test that matched my work energy. I like to take on big challenges and have a measurable way to track my results so I can feel the world's approval of my efforts. My plan to take a test each week and draw the results on a graph to chart my improvement was motivating for me. It fed my work energy, and it focused only on the 90% actions while ignoring all minor optimizations. That's the work energy formula, and it works every time.

Action Step Five: Design a Day Focused on 90% Activities, and Groundhog It Until Success

In previous action steps, you've identified your work energy and the type of work you want to apply it to. Then you decided the first step you could take to begin saving your first brick toward your goal.

Now, it's time to design a day that, if you groundhogged it enough times, would enable you to achieve your goal.

Suppose you want to become the top salesperson in your company. You attend a lot of meetings and do a lot of tasks each day, but you know the most high-value activity is simply calling contacts on your customer list. It's also the thing you put off the most because it's awkward and intimidating.

Put your work energy in the fight. You're a survivor? Walk into your boss's office and tell her if you don't achieve your goal this quarter, you don't deserve a promotion this year, but if you do, you'd like to talk with her about a raise and a more flexible work schedule. Your work energy is helpfulness? Change your calls to focus on your customers' problems and how you can solve the issues for them. Use your work energy.

Before you do anything else, buy a brick. Prove to yourself you're not a lazy lump of lard by picking up the phone immediately, pushing all excuses out of your mind, and simply talking to one contact.

Next, it's time to design a day that will achieve your goal. In addition to your normal work, listen to a sales podcast each morning to get you fired up and thinking about how you can sell. Instead of wasting an hour at lunch dreading when you have to go back to your desk, bring a brown bag lunch each day, lock your office door, and block off your calendar to stop all distractions. You simply call person after person for an hour straight, in between bites of your apple. Then, at the end of your day at 4:30 p.m., right before you go home, send a text to one person on your list and make one last call. Every day, simply groundhog that day until you succeed.

You've learned the secret. You already know more about achieving goals than most people will ever recognize in their lives. Most people will get lost in the minutiae of activities that are not essential to success. Most people spend their whole lives seeing opportunities but failing to go after them because they freeze up with intimidation when they aren't sure how to begin. They will never learn about designing the day and groundhogging that day until success.

The work energy formula will give you the upper hand on every goal you'll ever face. You only need to choose to move forward.

PART II
BARRICADES TO SUCCESS

6

WORKING ON THE WRONG THING

"We all want progress, but if you're on the wrong road, progress means doing an about-turn and walking back to the right road; in that case, the man who turns back soonest is the most progressive."
—C.S. Lewis

I started writing this book over four years ago, but I could never finish it. This book is 60% story and 40% lessons learned because I want it to be practical rather than theoretical. I knew I hadn't yet finished living the story I wanted to put in this book, and there was one life lesson I had to complete first.

The thing stopping me from finishing this book was my weight. Yep, it's time to get personal. Real personal. We're actually having a conversation about the cellulite circling my belly. How could I write a book with the subtitle *Finish Everything You Start and Fearlessly Take on Any Goal* while I knew full well that I was hiding the one goal that has always sneered at me—that knocked me over so many times I can't remember them all? If I really meant what I have said in this book, it was time for me to prove it to myself.

I'm not a blimp. I'm five feet ten inches and 220 pounds, with an average amount of muscle, a significant belly, and cheeks that resemble Santa Claus—although they aren't nearly as wonderfully rosy. Significantly over a healthy weight.

Years ago, on April 15, 2013, I committed to change. I remember the day specifically because I was at home sick, watching the news of the horrific

Boston Marathon bombing where three people died and more than a dozen lost limbs from the blast. I think it was the continuous news coverage of the marathon over the next few weeks, combined with feeling sick from the flu, that inspired me to get fit like those runners.

While a sane person would get fit by getting an exercise DVD, I put my work energy into the fight. I wanted to take on a big goal with a measurable result. Remember? "Look Ma! I can run a marathon too!"

I made two purchases. The first was a registration for the Top of Utah Marathon in Logan, Utah. As I was putting my ticket in my online shopping cart, I giggled to myself because I had a wonderfully devious idea. I'd buy two tickets instead and rope my wife into it. She's such a sucker.

My second purchase was the book *The Non-Runner's Marathon Trainer*[4] by David Whitsett. I literally just went to Amazon and typed "marathon" to see what stuff I should have, and the book popped up. I purchased the book the very next day after the Boston Marathon bombing: April 16, 2013.

Emily and I got a babysitter and went on our first "running date." We drove over to the local high school, put on our gym clothes, as I ignored the tag in my shirt which read XXL, and walked over to the starting line at the high school track. We wanted to get a baseline on how long it took us to run one mile so that we could know what pace to expect. At the time, we weren't doing any regular exercise.

I started the timer on my iPhone and set it down hastily so I wouldn't waste a second before I began to run. All we needed to do was accomplish four laps around the track—one mile. I remember thinking after the second lap that I was circling the drain of death, but I trudged on. At 10 minutes and 30 seconds, I fell across the finish line. It felt as if someone had taken a sledgehammer to my chest, and my lungs were filled with fire. I was sure my next cough would bring up my left lung. How had I allowed myself to get to such a state of poor physical fitness that one mile was so difficult to run? I shouldn't have even broken a sweat.

We spent a few weeks just pushing ourselves to get to two or three miles in a single run so we could begin a traditional marathon training schedule. The schedule we decided on was 13 weeks. The book we bought advocated running three short runs per week and one long run. During the three shorter runs, we just kept up our stamina and practiced increasing our pace. Then, one day a week, we'd push ourselves as hard as we could to increase our maximum distance. We had a plan that we could simply groundhog into success.

The runner's high is a real thing. I can't tell you how many people I've met who become addicted to running because of the sense of accomplishment they feel. Every morning, millions of people around the world wake up early, lace up their running shoes, put in earbuds, and run. I, personally, am not one of those people.

I despised every single run. All of them. I despised the way it made my lungs feel. I despised the exertion, the sweat, the pain, the exercise of will power, and I especially despised the dorky short-shorts the sport requires and the fact that I had to apply anti-chafing lubrication on my inner thighs. Embarrassing. Waking up early and greasing up my thighs to prance around in Richard Simmons's shorts until exhaustion was not a great way to get me feeling good about my body.

Oh, and I hate how public running is. Spending that many hours running around the streets near my home, everyone I knew saw me out there. I'm sure they thought, "Oh, how sweet. Chunky Jim thinks he's an athlete! And how brave of him to wear Richard Simmons's shorts!" Some of those onlookers were more discrete. They'd say things like "Hey, saw ya running yesterday. Looked like you were working really hard!"

"Um, yes. I was. I felt like I was dying. Thank you for asking. I do not look elegant, sophisticated, nor respectable when I run. Running is stupid. For the rest of my life, I will run from zombies and for no other cause. None at all."

I continued anyway. After all, I decided I'd groundhog this routine and I wasn't about to ruin the plot of the movie. Plus, as I've mentioned, I'm a sucker for any goal which allows me to compete with myself and track my progress with a number. If I'm honest, my main motivation was the picture I could post on Facebook of me finishing a marathon. My work energy is so childish. I could clearly see how far I ran each time and how long it took me to do it, so secretly I was in love with the goal at the same time that I despised it.

Emily and I kept up our marathon training schedule diligently. We took turns watching the kids while the other would go out and run. If we couldn't convince ourselves to get out in the morning, we'd force ourselves out in the afternoon even during the August heat. One of us would limp in the front door, red-faced and exhausted, and just fall down on the living room floor—unable to speak for a solid 20 minutes. That was the cue for the other person to lace up and head out on their run. We learned not to say things like "I'm back from my run, so it's your turn now," because those words were too agonizing to hear.

During the forming phase of our goal, we were all energy. We dreamed our goal and designed a day that we would groundhog until success. But the problems began during the long phase of training. The demons in your mind want you to stop and return to life as a lazy lump of lard.

The troubles hit after about seven weeks of marathon training. It was still extremely difficult, but we began feeling like we were on track to meet our goal. Being "on track" is often the most dangerous thing that can happen when working toward a goal. "On track" usually means a storm is coming.

When we see that we're "on track" and yet a tremendous amount of work is still required, it can be easy to let our willpower begin to relax. We silently tell ourselves, "Okay, all I have to do is continue and I'll get there." That's not the kind of attitude required to punch your legs forward after mile seven of a difficult run.

The storm came indeed. We skipped some runs. We ruined the plot of the movie and stopped groundhogging. We walked the last few miles of our long runs some days, and we didn't stick to the training schedule when we were traveling.

That's how "on track" so quickly turns into "far behind." Then, we see that we're far behind on reaching a difficult goal, and so we quit, thinking it's impossible.

It was only my work energy that kept me going. We had a ticket to run a marathon and I'd committed to the goal. We had to finish somehow.

In the book we'd purchased, I read one trick that helped. When I began to feel extremely exhausted and near the point of slowing my run to a walk, I told myself, "I've used up about 30% of my energy, and I'm more than halfway done with this run." Somehow, that trick really worked. I just viewed my energy as a metered amount on a scale and compared that scale to how many more miles were left to run. It made me feel like I could easily continue.

Yet we were far behind schedule. We had anticipated completing training runs of up to 21 miles before the marathon. Our thinking was that if we could run 21 miles in a practice, we could probably push ourselves the extra 5.2 miles in an actual marathon to finish the race.

Fourteen days before the marathon, we looked at the training calendar. We hadn't even come close to finishing what we'd planned. We ran our longest run to date—eight miles. At the end of the eight-mile run, we were completely spent. We had nothing left in the tank. But we were committed, so we continued.

Seven days before the marathon, we had one last chance at a long training run to push our max range. We determined on a Saturday morning I'd start at 5 a.m. and run as far as I could, then Emily would start as soon as I finished. Somehow, in a week, we needed to run 26.2 miles, but the furthest we'd ever gone up to that point was merely eight miles.

I drove over to Lake Lowell, only a few miles from our home, and parked the car. I wasn't looking forward to the run and consequently wasn't in a good mental state, so I foolishly hid the car keys in the little door that covers the gas cap. Yeah, the little door that *locks* when you close it. I was locked out of the car, so I figured I might as well just run a long time. There was no car to which I could return.

It was a perfect morning for running, with a nip in the air. I put in headphones and listened to audiobooks or podcasts for most of the run, switching to country music when I needed a boost of energy. I began running around the lake. The first five or six miles went by without much effort. I had done that many times before. Miles seven and eight were tougher, but I'd also done that, so I pushed through. I was determined to get a long run in since I was behind in my training schedule, so I pushed myself with sheer will through miles nine through 11. At mile 11, I was entirely gassed. I couldn't move another step. I had nothing left.

I called Emily to pick me up but she missed the phone call, so I just kept running. I eventually reached her: "I . . . can't . . . go . . . on. Pick me up!" I was 12 miles from home so it took her a while to reach me. By then, I'd reached 13 miles. I nearly collapsed when I fell into the car. I was so weak and exhausted and in pain. I had absolutely nothing left in the energy tank.

Emily went out on her run right after me. Her experience was nearly identical to mine. She called at 12 miles and by the time I picked her up, she had gone nearly 14. I had to make a quick stop by the local Thai restaurant before picking her up. It wasn't my fault! Thai curry was on the mind.

That was seven days before our marathon, where we were supposed to run 26.2 miles. A half marathon nearly killed us, yet seven days later, we needed to double our max capacity. It looked as though it would be nearly impossible.

I was discouraged. I'd put in so much work. Sure, I wasn't perfect. We had slacked off during the storm phase of the goal, but we'd come so far since that first one-mile run at the high school track. Now we were only seven days away from the race, and the furthest we could accomplish was only *half* of a marathon. Obviously, it would be impossible to double our range in seven days.

But I had committed to the goal. I had bought my ticket, and we were going to that race.

On the morning of the race, we stayed in a hotel near Logan, woke up at 5 a.m., and got on a bus with dozens of other runners to head up the mountain to the starting line. It was a crisp 45 degrees when the starting gun initiated the race. Another 913 people ran with us to complete the 26.2-mile torture.

I flew through the first 13 miles. I remember crossing the halfway point and being amazed that just seven days earlier, I was entirely spent at that distance. I continued running. At mile 15 I began to tire.

I repeatedly lied to myself about my internal energy tank: "Oh. I'm about 30% tired now. I have 70% of my energy left, and the race is more than half over, so I'm gonna make it."

Thinking of my energy reserves like a gas tank was the only way I could go on because intuitively I knew my body could be 100% capable of finishing the race. Tens of thousands of people finish marathons each year who are old, overweight, very young, etc. Knowing my body was capable, the problem with finishing was 100% mental. I had to force my mind to shut off and just allow myself to keep going without convincing myself to stop or turn back. Again, I must point out what running does to the mind— you talk to yourself as if you're another person and have arguments with yourself. It isn't right, and neither are those shorts.

I stopped at aid stations and sprayed this really awesome stuff on my thighs that felt cold and made them go numb. No idea what that magic potion was, but all the serious marathon runners seemed to use it a lot, so I indulged. Side note: do not spray said magic potion on your tongue out of curiosity. It will make it numb. Lesson learned.

At mile 21, I hit a wall. Runners understand "the wall" in a way that anyone who hasn't done it probably never will. One step you're tired but still going, and all of the sudden your legs just stop involuntarily. Suddenly you find yourself walking. You scream at your brain, "NO! As soon as I start walking, it's 10 times harder to get running again! Do not walk! Do not walk! We'll have to cover the same distance, but it will be much harder." And yet you walk.

I called Emily to tell her I just couldn't go on. I had nothing left in the tank. I'd lost track of her at some point during the race. I wasn't sure if she was ahead or behind me. She answered the phone with "I can't go on. I have nothing left." We both hit the wall.

If there had been a bus anywhere along the path at that point, I probably would have taken it. Both feet were bleeding in multiple spots. I had hit a point of complete mental exhaustion. I got so angry at my own mind from pushing myself to the max that I remember coming close to ripping out my earbuds and throwing my phone into a river as I crossed a bridge.

I couldn't tolerate even one more beat of motivating music! We were both entirely spent.

And yet we continued on. There really was no other option. Yes, we had hit a wall, but now our backs were against that wall and we were about to fight through it. We walked a mile, then got so angry at the race that we sprinted a mile, then jogged, then nearly crawled across the finish line. We finished the race in just over five hours, which was nearly three hours slower than the race winner.

Our months of training didn't suddenly turn us into runners. The excitement of the marathon did not even make me wonder if I'd ever want to run a marathon again. I knew I didn't. Running is painful and boring and I'd much rather play sports for exercise.

Yet the only way to describe the feeling of crossing that finish line with Emily was euphoria—more than just relief that we could stop running. It was euphoric.

I laid down on the grass in the park at the finish line and committed to simply lying there on that spot permanently. I still had a few months until winter, and I was sure I could order food from there. "Um, yes, I'd like to order two bowls of Thai curry? If you could please just bring them to my little spot on the grass near the finish line and insert each bowl into one of my giant Santa Claus cheeks, that'd be great. Okay, yeah, see you again at dinner time."

After an hour, I peeled myself up, took off my shoes, and wandered over to our car. We drove the two miles to the hotel and I laid down. Standing up to shower was entirely out of the question, so I must apologize to whomever the next hotel guest was in room 204. I'm sure they wash the sheets, but I'm not sure the sheets could have recovered from what I put them through.

As I closed my eyes, I honestly felt concerned that I might not wake up. That may sound like hyperbole. It was not.

It took 10 days for the soreness of the marathon to wear off but as time passed, I felt very proud of that medal. It was by far the most difficult physical thing I'd accomplished, and it gave me a sense that I could take on absolutely any goal in the future with the work energy formula.

In the ensuing years, I've often thought about the marathon training and wondered at what the human mind can do. Yes, the mind, not the body. Fourteen days before the marathon, the longest run I could do was eight miles despite exerting myself to the extreme. Seven days later, I ran 13 miles on those same legs. Another seven days later, I ran on those same legs, in that same body, in those same shoes, and went for 26.2 miles. How is that possible? Did I suddenly grow double the leg muscle in seven days to miraculously double my range? I seriously doubt that. Did my lungs or my heart suddenly double their capacity? Of course not.

The truth is that we all live in a space far, far from our capabilities. The Creator, our spiritual father, placed us on the earth with unlimited potential, and we allow ourselves to live far below our privileges.

While the marathon was empowering, it was not the end goal. The goal was to get down to a healthy weight. That day I was sick, lying on the couch watching the Boston marathon, I reached a breaking point where I was prepared to make sacrifices to achieve my goal.

After the soreness of the marathon wore off, I stepped on the scale and saw 220 pounds. I had not lost a single pound. Not one. How could this be possible?

I got a little smarter. I recognized that exercise alone simply did not provide an answer. I burned calories, but the exercise made me hungry, and without realizing it, I must have been eating more.

So I began focusing on consumption. I cut out all desserts and sugars and cut back on the portions I ate. This went on for months of working toward the goal. Still 220 pounds. No change.

I told myself that if I couldn't accomplish losing weight in two more months, I'd go to a doctor and get checked out to see what was wrong. The two months came and went, until I humbled myself and went in. The doctor tested me and got back with the results. My body was perfectly fine and nothing was keeping me from achieving a healthy weight.

The doctor prescribed a weight loss pill and promised it would help me lose weight, but the effect would only last two or three months, and then it would wear off and I'd have to do the hard work of maintaining it. I took the deal. I convinced myself I would have no problem whatsoever maintaining a lower weight. I just needed a jump-start. There's no way I'd allow myself to eat right through the pill and gain weight.

It worked incredibly well. I dropped nearly 30 pounds in three months. The pill simply stopped my appetite nearly entirely. I had no desire to eat. I stopped taking the pill when the doctor asked me to and focused all my effort on not gaining the weight back.

But I did. My weight skyrocketed over the next five months—placing me almost back to where I started. I was up to 207, which was only 13 pounds down from my starting point. I was able to maintain 207 for a few years comfortably.

I lost track of my goal, though. I have a digital scale that tracks my weight and allows me to see my historical weights going back 10 years. I gained about three pounds each year at a slow pace until I found myself right back at 220 pounds.

It was time for war. Nobody can out-willpower a goal like I can. I was not going to allow myself to be mediocre.

I decided it was time to begin lifting weights. Vast amounts of cardio in running a marathon was not a standalone answer. Unmitigated willpower in maintaining a quick pill-induced weight loss was also not an answer.

I determined that I needed a balanced approach. I needed to watch my caloric intake while simultaneously gaining muscle. If I gained muscle and built my body, it would use up more calories and make it much easier to maintain the weight loss when I got there.

I knew nothing about lifting weights, so I started shopping for a personal trainer. I read the websites of every personal trainer within a 20-mile radius of my home and settled on one with pages of inspiring testimonials with before-and-after pictures.

I laughed because I'd taken so many "before" pictures over the previous four years. There's so much hope in a before picture, but then six months later I would take *another* "before" picture as I began the *next* round of diet or exercise that would surely be the silver bullet.

I walked into the office of my personal trainer for the first day. I didn't have to swallow my pride—I had to gag on it as I crammed it down my throat. It was really hard walking in there—60 pounds overweight—past the other superhuman weightlifters to the office of my personal trainer to ask for help. Most of their clients were preparing for competitions, and there came Santa Claus-cheeks to try and burn off his Twinkies.

Other than the more pinkish shade of skin, the trainer very closely resembled the Hulk. He was a towering mass of lumps of muscle. He was about six foot three. Oh, funny, you thought I meant he was six feet three inches tall? No, no. That was the circumference of just one of these dude's biceps. The man was an impressive physical specimen.

I sat down in his office and unloaded everything. The marathon, the pills, the unmitigated willpower, the calorie tracking, everything. I just wanted the change, and I would do exactly what he told me to do to get there. I'd pay him whatever it takes.

I signed the contract for a very expensive personal training program. He'd create a precise meal plan for me and stand right beside me for every single rep of weightlifting until I reached my goal. We were in this together.

Two days later, I returned for my first workout. I had never done any real weightlifting before, so he had to show me every single step. I remember the first time I laid down on the bench to do dumbbell chest presses and I couldn't figure out how to lift the heavy weights into position on my chest. They were too heavy to lift up to my chest from the lying position. I looked up at my trainer after three or four attempts and he had a most amused and bewildered look. Eventually, I stood back up and used the momentum of me falling onto the bench to swing the weights up into position on my chest and catch them.

Seeing this, the Hulk said, "That was the most ridiculous and dangerous way I've ever seen anyone move a dumbbell."

Nice. Way to make Santa feel welcome. Apparently, when you sit down on the bench, you're supposed to rest the dumbbells on your knees and then kick up your knees to push them up to your chest after laying down. Who knew? I thought my toss-the-weight-and-catch-it method was pretty clever, though admittedly ineffective.

Wall sits, lunges, chest presses, and Romanians—the stupid names for the torturous exercises only added insult to my pain. After my first one-hour weightlifting session, I felt weak in the knees as I slowly hobbled out to my car. I sat down in the front seat of my aging Nissan Sentra and immediately the windshield fogged up from my hot, sweaty, giant Santa Claus cheeks. I looked in the rearview mirror at myself and blood was pouring from my nose. It was the first bloody nose I'd had since I was a child. I exerted myself to a breaking point. I just sat there in my car for 20 minutes before I felt that I could drive home. I was absolutely going to achieve my goal, and it wouldn't be a lack of exertion on my part that kept me from it.

The workouts didn't get any easier over time, and the soreness didn't subside in time for the next workout to come. I had to take ibuprofen every single day to push through the pain.

Because my primary goal was weight loss, my trainer set up a routine optimized for that. He hadn't worked with overweight people before, since most of his business was focused on preparing people for bodybuilding competitions, but he felt confident he knew what I should do. Instead of eight to twelve reps of each lift like a traditional weightlifting routine, we would do four sets of 40 reps for each lift, with a generous three-to-five-minute pause between lifts. I would also raise my calories significantly to provide fuel for muscle growth.

No matter what the personal trainer asked of me, I gave 110%. I gave all of myself for many months. I was shocked at how much work it was, but I knew I would reach my goal. The Hulk obviously knew how to get fit, so I could trust him, right?

It took me eight months of the most grueling physical labor of my life, but the day finally came that I stepped on the scale, nervously looked down at the numbers, and read the same weight as I had before starting the program: 220.

I was completely shattered, but I knew the scale didn't tell the whole story, so I pulled out my before picture and compared it to the after. The "after" picture looked like a photocopy of the "before." My arms looked the same, my chest looked the same, there was the tiniest little lump of muscle in my calves, but other than that I looked precisely identical to the "before" picture. I was still the same weight and appeared to have the same amount of fat. How was it possible?

After a few very frustrating months, I finally got the gumption to try again. This time, at the recommendation of my sister-in-law, I tried a meal delivery service. I was interested in the concept of having five delivered meals a day so that I didn't have to choose what to eat. It was all there in a box for me. I could just grab one of the packages, rip it open, eat, and know I was on track. Simple. Then, one meal a day, I'd eat a piece of chicken and some broccoli. Dead simple. I read about it online and watched all the YouTube videos and was getting excited about it.

Then I went to order the meal service and stopped. I saw on their website that it was an MLM (multilevel marketing business, where the company has sellers who make commissions not only for their sales but for the salespeople they recruit to the business). I hate MLMs. Oh, no. I just said the dreaded acronym. My wife knows that I can't resist going on my MLM tangent. I see it all the time. Emily is constantly getting invited to a "party" one of her friends is throwing. The women show up, and then the host introduces her "really successful friend who drives a Mustang and is going to show us her cute jewelry business." Argh. I'd rather drive a pencil through my eye.

I digress, but only to explain my disgust when I found out this was an MLM. But my sister-in-law, who was *not* selling the stuff, had given me a good review of the service, so I was interested. I swallowed my MLM aversion and called my local "coach." Ugh, I hated that they were called coaches. I would have felt much better about it if they were just called salespeople. Anyway, I called my coach/salesperson.

It didn't take me long on the phone with my new salesperson to change my mind. She said something that stuck with me. She asked me how long I'd been overweight, and the story of how I got to the point that I called her. I told her that I had tried and tried so many different things and that

I was a hard worker and had really pushed myself, but just couldn't find what worked for my body.

She said, "Yes, we'll need to figure out exactly what works for your body, but more importantly, I want to know why you've allowed yourself to get unhealthy in the first place, and why you allowed yourself to remain unhealthy for so many years."

That hurt to hear, but I knew the question was only pointed because it was on point. The answer was that I had simply convinced myself that I was doing my best that whole time. In reality, I just hadn't committed to 90% of the work. Yes, I nearly died in my bed after running a marathon and survived months of abuse from the Hulk, but that's an optimization of the body compared to the most important part—regulating food intake, which achieves 90% of the result.

I fully committed to the program. All I had to do was wait for the box of food to come, open it up, and eat five of their snacks each day, then eat a piece of chicken and broccoli for dinner. I had to swallow my pride when they insisted on calling the snacks "fuelings" and hearing the marketing people in the videos use the phrase "gentle, fat-burning state" every-other sentence. It drove me nuts, but I was committed and I wouldn't break. I also didn't like it when my health coach texted me and "checked in" to see how I was doing, but over time I actually found her to be very encouraging and helpful.

My weight began to plummet. I was hangry. Oh, believe me, I was hangry. "Gentle, fat-burning state" was completely the wrong phrase to describe how I felt. I felt like my body was eating itself as I wasted away, dying in the desert for want of food. For the first 18 days, I felt constantly on the verge of losing my patience at people around me with no provocation. It was all I could do to resist grabbing my kids' crackers as I passed them on the kitchen counter. Then things changed. My body adapted, and my mind adapted. On day 19 of my journaling, I noticed that I didn't really feel hungry, my energy was back, and it wasn't difficult to turn down other foods.

I was absolutely perfect on that diet. No days off, no cheating. And you know what? It worked. I'm now a healthy 175 pounds—down 35 pounds from the 220-pound starting weight. I went from a size 38 waist to a size 32. I wore an XX-large T-shirt and now I wear a medium. I still have a slight muffin top and pooch, but I am at a healthy weight and moving in the right direction.

I have learned so much about health over the last few years. I learned what didn't work. I learned cardio is helpful but by no means sufficient. I learned that counting calories is really tough to do accurately and that meal plans on the internet are usually wrong, since I followed so many without losing a pound.

I learned that my personal trainer was either inept or lazy. Looking back, I realize that I was incredibly sore without reaching my goals because of the routine he had chosen. We'd do 35-40 reps in four sets frequently. That's very far off the mark of what most knowledgeable trainers would do. It was probably because he just didn't want to rearrange the gym and set up a new machine to move to new lifts more frequently. I learned that training when incredibly sore is rather pointless because the muscle is already torn and needs time to properly heal. I learned that the meal plan I was given may have been great for someone with a significant amount of muscle but was a terrible idea for my body.

More than anything, I learned something about motivation that I had never realized. While not all of the plans I'd made were successful, I was able to follow some of them perfectly, and others not at all. Since my primary work energy is overcoming hard things to get praise, I needed a plan that I could feel convinced would lead me to success if I merely followed it. To other people, that doesn't work at all. If they see all of the work ahead of them that needs to be done, they feel intimidated and shrink immediately. For me, just trying to track my own calories and setting my own caloric intake goals failed because I wasn't sure I was right on the numbers. The more specific the program was and the more confidence I had that it was the most efficient path—even if it was far more difficult than other plans—the more I was able to follow it. I needed to be motivated in the right way for myself.

Because my work energy is achievement and I thrive on accomplishing things and want people to be proud of me, it was actually better for me to have an intimidating and difficult plan so I could, in the end, say, "Look at me, Ma!"

Yes, I know it sounds childish, but that's my work energy. In the end, something deep down inside me must be looking for praise even though I don't recognize it. If you think about it, though, all of our work energies seem childish on the outside.

So what finally worked for me? I focused on the one thing that gave me 90% of the result. I didn't even exercise at all while dieting. I simply ate less food on a strict schedule. I focused 100% of my energy on reducing my food intake and that got me 90% of the way there. Then, once the weight was lost, I could focus 100% of my energy on what's needed now—not looking "skinny fat" but gaining some muscle definition.

Once I had identified the one action that would get me 90% of the way there, I simply groundhogged that day until success. I had the five 100-calorie snacks each day, then a small meal of chicken and veggies for dinner. I repeated that day until I reached success. Because I had correctly identified the 90% action of regulating food intake, I saw rapid progress and thus, maintaining the daily action was easy. It's easy to work hard when you see rapid progress.

You may read this chapter and argue with my plan. You may be far more fit than I am and know a lot more about optimizing weight loss and health than I do. That's the problem, however. I was trying to optimize things by going the extra mile and running a marathon, lifting weights with the Hulk while I was losing weight, and using pills and supplements to expedite the process. There is not a thing wrong with any of those things, but optimizations should never be implemented during the groundhog phase of a goal when you just need to get the bulk of the result. Once you've achieved 90% of the goal, it will likely take optimizations to achieve the last 10%.

I include this chapter in the book not to completely embarrass myself by talking about thigh greasing, short shorts, and my belly. I include it to warn you about focusing your effort on the wrong thing.

What's the Right Thing?

Before you can design a day and groundhog it into success, you must first be absolutely certain that the day contains no "good ideas" or "optimizations." Only focus on the most crucial aspect of the work that will achieve 90% of the result. Do not forget or stop your groundhog day once you've achieved 90% of the result and need to begin focusing on optimizations for the remaining 10% of the goal.

If you want to win a local election, focus only on personally speaking to as many people as you can. The design of your yard signs, debate prep, flyers, raising funds, and everything else can wait.

> *Focus only on the action that achieves*
> *90% of the result.*

If you want to climb Everest, put on a 100-pound pack and hike up the steepest hill in your city each morning before work while wearing an altitude mask. Studying routes, choosing your guide, fretting over which ice axe to choose, and all other considerations can wait until you reach the optimization period—after you've achieved 90% of the goal.

If you want to buy a bigger house, focus only on saving the big $500 chunk each month instead of worrying about saving $2 on a smoothie here and there. You can scrimp and save every last penny, but if it drives you crazy and pushes you to fall off the horse and book a $5,000 vacation, it won't amount to much.

My brother Paul ran an Ironman race a few years ago. After a 2.4-mile swim in frigid water, he raced to the changing tent to get off his wet suit and put on his dry clothes. His hands were so cold and he was so tired that he was shaking uncontrollably, trying to get the zipper down on his suit. An older man walked up to him and put his hand on Paul's shoulder.

He said, "Son, I've run over 20 of these races. I'll tell you one thing. You are not going to win this race. Focus on finishing. So sit down there for five minutes in the warm tent and get your temperature back up."

At first, he was taken aback by the lack of confidence the man had in him, but he soon realized it was true. This was a 15-hour race and 30 seconds of fumbling with a zipper would not catapult him onto the podium. His mission was to finish. By ignoring the optimization of fumbling with his zipper and pushing through the cold, he was able to calm down and focus on simply finishing the race. If he'd pushed himself to optimize for every second, it still wouldn't have put him on the podium, and he may not have even finished the race.

Action Step Six: Identify Potential Optimizations of Your Goal (and Skip Them!)

Set aside all optimizations until you have achieved 90% of the success. Re-evaluate the 90% action to ensure it will accomplish the correct result.

Write a list of all of the actions you could take to help you achieve your goal. Identify which action is the most vital to get you to your goal. Then separate out all of the optimizations into another section to work on only after you've achieved 90% of your result.

Here is an example: John is 35 and unmarried. He feels it is time for him to settle down and start a family. He has dated plenty of girls but hasn't yet found the right one.

John makes a list of all of the actions he could take to help him reach his goal: get involved in community organizations to meet women, lose weight, become financially stable, go dancing on Friday nights, go out with friends more often, get some new clothes to look better, save up for a wedding ring, go on dates.

We can debate which action is most important, but John feels that he spends plenty of time hanging out with groups of people. Going on actual one-on-one dates is the most important thing he could do. John then designs a day to achieve his goal. Each day on his lunch break, he will text at least two women he wouldn't normally text. On Tuesdays he'll start attending a singles group he found on Facebook, and over the entire week he'll work toward finding a date for Saturday night. Because he's been texting people all week, that shouldn't be too tough. Going on actual dates is the thing he's determined will get him 90% of the way there. Now John simply groundhogs that goal until success.

All of the other items on his list, like saving up for a ring and becoming financially stable, are good things to optimize, but they are likely to divert his attention from the most important action—going on dates. John gets 90% of the way there, and then in the finishing phase he can work on the other optimizations to prepare him for marriage and starting a family. It wouldn't help John to get married if he got a job at night delivering pizzas to save up for a wedding ring and never even met the girl he wanted to marry.

7

VISIONARY POISON

At this point, you have the complete work energy formula. Understand your work energy and your barricades, dream a goal, identify only the most vital actions that will drive 90% of the result and that match your work energy, then groundhog the goal until success. Those steps will empower you to crush goals that the vast majority of people will never achieve. Yet success isn't quite that simple.

The entirety of Part II of this book focuses on overcoming the common problems that pop up as you follow the work energy formula. Anyone can tell you to get on a good diet and keep dieting until you're skinny, but that wouldn't solve your problem, would it? The truth is most goals are incredibly simple. The work energy formula will get you to where you need to be, but the trouble is the work energy formula is being implemented by a lazy lump of lard. By that, I mean a human being who, by nature, does not want to break into unknown territory.

You may think that you simply need to be more disciplined to achieve your goals. That's not the answer either. Your mind has a few tricks that it loves to play on a disciplined mind to slow it down just the same, and the rest of this book will help you learn the tactics to overcome that issue.

When you have a path before you to achieve a goal, it's easy to put your head down and miss signs of trouble ahead. That's what happened to me.

My business began to grow. By the end of the next year, we brought in $234,000. The year after that, we earned $360,000.

I wanted to scale the business up further—because that's what successful CEOs do, right? The income of $30,000 per month was steady and it provided so much money for my family that we didn't always know what to spend it on, other than to simply continue saving.

Somehow, the lawyer job still seemed to be the safer route, and I felt fear each day about the business dying out. Perhaps it would have helped me to realize that over 20% of those with a job have experienced a layoff in the previous five years,[5] according to the John J. Heldrich Center for Workforce Development at Rutgers University. Having a job may not actually be a more secure source of income than starting a business.

With a large income and no debt, we could have purchased a massive home if we had accepted a mortgage. The temptation was certainly there, but Emily and I have always felt that security for our family was worth more than any amount of financial leverage. We had satisfied our family's needs through the simple daily action of publishing new content. Now, I was ready to take on the 10% of optimization in the business to hit the next level.

At the beginning of the next year, I sat down with a pen and paper to lay out a growth strategy. I carefully crafted a plan to expand. My business plan had four goals:

1. Expand into areas of the photography market other than just teaching photography.
2. Create three additional online courses.
3. Create a full-fledged video studio to make video production of courses and other videos faster.
4. Hire an additional employee to handle accounting and customer service so I could focus on new growth.

Little did I know that those were literally the four worst possible courses of action I could have taken at that time. Those four line items that seemed like such a solid plan sent us into an unexpected tailspin that nearly brought the company down. I had no idea my plan was a cliff, and I was driving my small business straight for it—as fast as I could.

Business books and podcasts were poisoning me. While I'd benefited greatly for years in learning from them, I began to *chase their* ideas rather than to be merely inspired by them as I acted on my own. It's what I've come to refer to as "visionary poison." I would read a book about Elon Musk or Steve Jobs. "They had such vision! When all the rest of the auto industry was stuck in an old mindset, he completely re-envisioned what the automobile could become." Or "His foresight was incredible! He took complicated devices and made them simple and premium."

Then I'd walk into work and what would I do? "Dustin! We're going to design and manufacture our own camera! Look, this is a multibillion-dollar market! The interface on rear LCD screens of cameras still looks like MS-DOS and I think we could do something revolutionary here. We are earning $30,000 a month and have some cash that we could use to create a minimum viable product and launch something on Kickstarter. We're making a camera!"

A week later, I'd walk in and say, "Dustin! I have a great idea! Creating these videos is taking a long time. What if we invest $20,000 into creating a full-fledged TV studio right here in the office to up our game?"

It was visionary. Frankly, it was entirely possible. But it so diverted us from what had proven successful in the business up to that point that it began to erode our core business. Is it possible for a little upstart to upend the camera business? Of course it's possible.

So far, I'd flipped the statistics on their head. One out of every five small businesses lasts 20 years. I'd already survived three years, so if I simply kept reinforcing our successes and slowly growing, I could have a fantastic and dependable business. Yet I was chasing after the type of one-in-a-million success that only a few visionaries succeed in. I'd traded one in five for one in a million.

That's where most business books seem to place their focus—the one-in-a-million shot that actually paid off. The iPhones, Teslas, and search engines that we literally only see once or twice a decade. It's as if we focused all of the attention in our public schools on raising every kid to be the President of the United States. Of course, it's awesome to become the president, but it's such a long shot that it would lead our kids into missing excellent opportunities to be small business owners, computer engineers, florists, accountants, doctors, and businesspeople.

It's visionary poison. I really admire Elon Musk. He's an absolutely incredible, visionary CEO and an asset to the world. Yet if I were to try and act like Elon Musk in my business, I guarantee the company would be bankrupt within five years. He has the visionary poison and it has pushed him to take unfathomable risks with his companies over the years, but he has that one-in-a-million ability to pull it off. I think Elon Musk actually is the once-in-a-generation leader who can achieve any vision, but for mere mortals like me, I'll pass on the visionary poison.

The truth is that small business owners don't need the one-in-a-million success to be successful. I was earning $30,000 per month as a recent law grad. I have a wonderful wife and at the time I had two children. I owned my home outright and was excited about getting to work every day. I didn't need to be a visionary. Frankly, I wouldn't even want that kind of life. Yet the allure of the visionary poison tainted my business objectives.

The fact is that most entrepreneurs will never reach the visionary success of the famous, once-a-decade companies, and the over-attention we give these successes keeps the majority of people from starting a business that could change their lives.

My goals were about expansion when they should have been about reinforcement. Visionaries expand constantly and rarely take time to reinforce. Small business owners who stand the test of time spend most of their efforts in reinforcement. You have identified the actions needed to achieve 90% of the success toward your goal.

> *When you reach the top of that hill and are ready to optimize the last 10%, ensure first that your optimizations won't distract you from continuing the 90% actions.*

When I was a kid growing up in Hawaii, I built a *lot* of sandcastles. The trick to building sandcastles is getting the sand wet. If you form up the right consistency of sand and water in a bucket and place it on the castle, it will stick. The sand sticks and so you continue building up and around. Just as you turn your attention to the next part of the castle, you look back to see your work crumbling. Why? Because the spot was not reinforced. Without a sufficiently thick wall, the water drains out and the castle crumbles. Each spot needs to be reinforced before another area can be worked on.

My highly successful small business was a sandcastle, and I couldn't see it at the time. Revenue had grown nearly every month since the day I started tapping out words on my netbook two years earlier.

Let's review again my four goals for the year:

1. Expand into areas of the photography market other than just teaching photography.

2. Create three additional online courses.

3. Create a full-fledged video studio to make video production of courses faster.

4. Hire an additional employee to handle accounting and customer service so I could focus on new growth.

Expanding into new areas of photography was the last thing I should have been doing. I didn't realize how perilous my position in the market was for my core business that would soon be at risk. That goal was tainted with visionary poison.

The next goal was to expand our online course offerings. We had only one course, and I wanted to expand to five online courses. This project would take nearly 100% of our time for five months when we should have focused on diversifying our marketing so we weren't too reliant on Facebook.

Our one online course for beginning photographers was selling for $99. It was bringing in 70% of the company's revenue. The most logical decision was to create a second online course. We did, and revenue jumped up an additional $12,000 the next month to crest the $40,000 mark. Success! So what did we do that next month? Create another online course! Another jump! Quickly, we had an expansive line of online courses.

Yet the jumps faded. After a few months, revenues landed back at $30,000. One good product plus one more good product does not equal two revenues. We still sold to the same number of customers, but now they had more options for a course that more closely fit their skill level. On top of that, we started getting an onslaught of customer service inquiries asking what course they should choose as they weren't sure if they were a beginner or intermediate photographer. Customer confusion likely turned many potential customers away.

The excitement we'd generated for the online courses also started to dim. When the month started and we'd announce the new session of the course, we now had to change the marketing. Now, five new courses were opening up. With five times the available open spots in courses, they stopped selling out. The urgency of "this course always sells out within minutes" was removed from our marketing messages.

It took time for me to see what was happening and why our efforts had not resulted in additional revenue. Income was still steady, but I had unknowingly thrown a grenade on our marketing campaign.

Yet we had come so far and created so many great new courses that I couldn't back down. The thought didn't even cross my mind to go back to one simple, successful offer and just work on reinforcing it with marketing.

Traffic to the website was holding steady at over 300,000 pageviews per month with great consistency because the articles I'd written in the previous year were still ranking on Google and sending traffic from Pinterest. I stopped writing new content for the website so I could focus on our product offerings, which just weren't quite selling as I'd hoped. Remember the sandcastle? I was allowing our most important asset—traffic to the website—to dry and crumble as I worked on another area of the sandcastle.

The problem was visionary poison—constantly trying to expand the business instead of spending most of my efforts reinforcing what has proven to work. In an effort to expand, I stopped writing the daily blog posts, which were driving 90% of the results for my business, so I could focus on the 10% of optimizations.

If I had focused on writing more and more content on the website, I could have more and more articles leading people to ImprovePhotography.com and the offering we had. I had already proven tremendous success came from writing more content on the website, so why did the visionary poison in me want to try out new and unproven methods to expand the company?

I was about to pay a price for that lesson.

The dip began. The numbers that had fueled my work energy were now working against it. We dropped to $28,000 a month, $25,000 a month, then $18,000 a month. The blood ran cold through my veins and I couldn't think about anything else the day I saw that profit and loss statement with $18,000 at the top. Where had my business gone?

My dream was to free my family from the constraints of money, but my old fear was back to haunt me.

What I can clearly see now but did not understand at the time was that courses were being sold to new people we brought in each month. To someone who had followed the website for a year, they had already had dozens of opportunities to sign up for a course and thus our marketing efforts to reach them were unlikely to succeed. I either needed to put a completely different offering in front of them (something other than yet another online course), or I needed to bring in far more new customers to see our offerings. At the same time, I was competing with YouTube, which was becoming more popular with dozens of free videos teaching the very basics of photography that I was teaching in my course.

At the time, however, I had no idea what was wrong. All I knew was sales were down even though we had done so much expansion work.

The dip continued. We pushed our social media posts harder and harder to encourage people to take an online photography class with us, but this became overaggressive and annoying to potential customers—making the decision not to purchase a course firmer in their minds.

One month the revenue hit $16,000 and I was nearly ready to curl up in the fetal position in the corner of the office. I had hired an office manager only five months previous and now I could see that if nothing changed soon, I wouldn't be able to justify having employees—or paying for that orange carpet.

I saw this all the time with new photographers who dreamed of eventually turning pro. When they first start learning, they take their camera everywhere. They take pictures at the kid's soccer game, they wake up early while on vacation to learn landscape photography, and they eat up learning the fundamentals of exposure. Then, they decide to optimize.

They decide they need a better camera. They get wrapped up in following the rumors sites to see when the newest model will be released and learn to read MTF charts for finding the sharpest lenses possible. Suddenly, they look up and realize they haven't picked up a camera in months, and their skills have grown stagnant. Their goal of turning pro is no closer than before they began to optimize.

It was the "good idea" to get a new camera that ruined the progress. You had it in the bag! You were learning the fundamentals and, most importantly, simply taking pictures each day. It was working. If you would have simply stuck to groundhogging your goal, you would be there. Then, once your pictures were at a professional level, you could add some optimizations to help you turn pro without stopping the simple but important act of taking pictures daily.

The same thing is true with every goal. When you design your day and begin groundhogging, you must stop having good ideas. Do not optimize, adjust the plan to match your schedule, change the day to get even faster results, etc. You analyzed what worked for you, identified the effort that would result in the fastest progress, and you've been doing it. Stop. Do not add visionary poison into your goal.

In my business, I got 90% of the result by simply writing one new blog post each day to bring new people in the door. Yet I was wasting time creating memes on Facebook to drive engagement, creating multiple courses instead of one great one, being a visionary CEO, building a camera, etc. This visionary poison accumulated so quickly that I looked up one day and realized it had been many months since I'd published a new post on my blog. How could it have happened?

Know that "good ideas" will come to you once you design your day and begin seeing success. Do not listen to Siren's song. If you change anything as you groundhog your designed day, the plot of the movie will be ruined.

Action Step Seven: Identify the Visionary Poison in Your Path

This step seems so easy. You don't even need to do anything. You simply have to *not* do something: just don't have any good ideas. That's it. Yet you'll almost certainly find that this step is more difficult than any other.

You looked at yourself and determined your work energy. You took an initial step to get the fire burning in your bones and then began groundhogging the action that is most important to get you to your goal. You are on the right path right now.

You get the point. The best way to ruin your best success is to come up with a better idea.

This is probably the first and last time you'll be told to stop having good ideas, but seriously. Stop having good ideas. When you set up a groundhog day, you cannot change that day until you succeed.

Here are a few tips to help you stop having good ideas:

1. Watch old episodes of Star Trek or baseball.
2. Eat a dozen donuts and drown them in a liter of chocolate milk.
3. Spend an evening reading the setup instructions for a piece of furniture from Ikea.

Don't cheat on your groundhog day. Put yourself in a loop that doesn't end until success. The movie would have stunk if Bill Murray could take a break from Groundhog Day at any point because he felt like living Saint Patrick's Day instead. You are locked in. The only way to let yourself out of Groundhog Day is reaching the goal.

Don't let visionary poison corrupt your path.

8

THE LIMITS OF OUR OPTIMIZATIONS

> *"Deep in his heart, every man longs for a battle to fight, an adventure to live, and a beauty to rescue."*
> —John Eldredge

In business, my greatest weakness is my "ready, fire, aim" mentality. I get an idea and go after it like a rocket before taking important preparatory steps. That weakness sometimes slows the steady growth of my work in business, but when there is an emergency in the business and a decision has to be made with imperfect information and few resources, that weakness is my greatest asset.

While in hindsight I can see the problem of visionary poison clouding my business and causing catastrophic results, I didn't understand what was happening at the time. I took a few days at home away from the office to think things through. I just needed to reset and figure it all out. No clear answer came. I had done everything right according to what I'd learned. I never sat complacently—I had expanded like crazy.

All I saw was that our traffic was consistent, we had far better products, and yet far fewer customers were buying. Without an answer, there was only one path forward. If I couldn't increase revenue, I had to cut expenses—to the bone. Emily and I prayed, worried, and stressed, but the only conclusion we could find was that I would have to walk onto the orange carpet and tell my employees they were being laid off. How could this have happened?

I walked in on a Monday morning and sat down with my little team. I met with them individually and told them I simply couldn't justify the expense of employees and an office when the business was shrinking. I gave them as much notice as possible and gave as much severance as I could possibly afford, but I told them I had to let them go.

When they left the office that morning, I broke down in tears. I was completely alone in that office with no answers as to how to fix the problem. I let my team down. My dream was slipping from my grasp. My business had become what I was known for, and it was disappearing. I stuck my neck out and went rogue from law, and now I had a shell of a business left.

I had too much pride to admit to friends and family what was happening. I said things like "We're still making great money, but we realized that having the extra employees just isn't giving us an ROI (return on investment)." It was true—kind of. But the truer truth was something I couldn't admit to anyone else.

I felt like a failure because the shrinking business critically damaged my work energy. I wanted to appear successful in front of others. "Look Ma! I tried a business and failed catastrophically!" This hit me harder than it may have for others.

I took a selfie in front of the door to the office that day after the office emptied. It was the very lowest day of my entire life, but for some reason, I knew I wanted to remember it. Somehow I knew I'd look back and say, "Remember that? It all looked so bleak that day." It *was* bleak that day. There was no light at the end of the tunnel. There were no more solutions to consider. I had no idea how to get out of the box I'd put myself in.

The very next day, I came into the office alone. I turned down the thermostat and put on a coat to save some money, as if that would save me. I mostly stared at the computer and wondered what all those numbers were trying to tell me about where I had failed.

Around 10 a.m., I heard the squeak of the tiny metal mail slot in the front door open, and a few letters slid through. I flipped through the mail and found a blue-rimmed Christmas card with a nice picture of a blue jay on the front. I curiously turned it around and found these words handwritten on the back:

"Dear Jim. It might be a little strange for me to be sending you a Christmas card since you don't know me, but I took your photography course this year and it helped me to take better pictures. The picture of the bird on the front of this card is one of my favorites I took this year. Just wanted to let you know that your work is making a difference. Merry Christmas. —Charlene Dumas"

I've never met Charlene, and she'll be surprised to see her name in this book if she ever happens to read it, but she could not have done a kinder thing for me at that moment. I still have the card. You'll recall that my work energy is fed when I achieve difficult things so I can feel the praise of that effort being accepted or admired by others. With the numbers in my business lagging, which had always been the thing that drove me forward, I was especially low. Praise was what fed my work energy, and this Christmas card was just the medicine I needed.

I still had two months remaining on the lease of the building, so I continued working from the orange carpet instead of working from home. My desk sat in a large 20-by-30-foot space—right in the middle with nothing else in the room. Nothing on the walls, no people in the other rooms of the office—just me, working 10 to 12 hours a day, in an empty, musty office in historic Nampa, Idaho. Trains passed by regularly and shook the walls, but I barely noticed as I focused my attention on my keyboard.

I determined my best path forward was to come up with a new product type unaffected by the grenade I'd thrown into our marketing of the online courses.

It was August. I could see Black Friday on the horizon, which is the biggest shopping day of the year in the United States.

My plan was to come up with a product so good that customers *had* to buy. I would turn on every marketing trick I had ever learned. The offer would be time-limited for only 48 hours. The product would be something that would show well in a video sales pitch, and I'd send tremendous traffic to the sales page.

I put together my offer. I created several bundles of presets for Lightroom. These are photo filters for serious photographers. Each bundle of 20 presets would normally be $40, but I included multiple bundles and added a webinar, a new photography course, and more. I made the entire package $40. It would normally cost over $1,000 to get all of the digital items individually after the sale had ended. I figured if that didn't sell, nothing would sell.

Bleak is the only word I can think of to describe that time. I was depressed in a way I'd never been before. In hindsight, I really should have met with a doctor as I was barely able to function. I was so exhausted I felt I couldn't get up in the morning. The only thing keeping me going was the encouragement of Emily and the possibility of this new Black Friday sale. That was the only time in my life where I could say I was truly depressed. Like everyone, I have my own struggles and downtimes, but looking back, this was more than that.

The greatest stress for me was the loss of who I was. I had been a poor law student. I was known to family and friends as the one who went rogue and started a company. I was so proud of that little company's growth; just about everyone I knew had seen me as a success. My company had become an essential part of the story of who I told myself I was. Now that story was one of failure, I couldn't shake it. There was a very real possibility that the best days of my career were behind me already.

I have heard many entrepreneurs talk about not letting your company become your identity, and I then understood what they meant. I didn't even realize it had happened, but the company's story was my story. Intuitively I knew I was more. My family, my faith, and my friends meant more to me than money, but it was the story of failure writing itself within me that affected me so deeply.

Don't Let Success or Failure Define You

I learned the importance of not allowing failure *or* success to define me. Writing these stories in your mind is dangerous. The story of failure says success does not come to you. The story of success says failure does not come to you. But every life will see both. I found that to be truly resilient, I needed to rewrite my story to be a phrase I once heard: "I've come through some tough spots in the past, but somehow I always seem to make it through." It is neither success nor failure—it's a story of resiliency.

I spent months working tirelessly in the echoey office. I was relentless. Now with very few expenses for the company, the business was earning more than enough to meet our needs, but it was the failure story that I had to rewrite. It wasn't all about pride, though. I saw my business cut to less than half of what it was doing before in a matter of four months. If it happened again, I wouldn't know what to do. I couldn't allow that failure story to finish itself or I knew I'd never get out.

It was two days until Black Friday. I opened the creaky door to walk onto the orange carpet again. (To be fair, it wasn't solid orange. There were flecks of yellow and dark brown in it.) I spent 14 hours recording take after take of my sales video for my Black Friday flash deal. It had to be flawless. I recorded it so many times that now even many years later, I can almost do it by memory. You can go back on YouTube and hear the whole pitch: "Hey photo nerds. If you're like me, you've taken lots of pictures that look okay, but you just can't quite get it to that professional level . . . "

Black Friday. I woke up at midnight to press the launch button. I pressed "publish" on my carefully crafted sales video, I switched the yellow "buy now" button to the live link to the shopping cart, and I was open for business. I posted everywhere. I plastered it all over the website. I put up ads on Facebook and Google. I created YouTube videos. I did everything I could to get that message to the masses.

It felt as if my entire career was dependent on the next hour.

It all reminds me of when I was a kid on the morning of Hurricane Iniki. The storm was coming, the warning sirens were blaring along our street, which was steps away from Pearl Harbor. The military police drove up and down our neighborhood telling everyone to get out. Something was coming and we had no idea what it would be.

That's how I felt. But rather than binge-watching the local news for weather information, I was refreshing my PayPal account as fast as I could press F5. First nothing, then that satisfying notification of the first sale.

Sales poured in with the ferocity of a hurricane. Within an hour—in the middle of the night—the sale had already brought in a few thousand dollars. I drove home in a blind numbness and slept for a few hours before rushing back to a computer to refresh.

The sale was not going well; it was going unbelievably well! Thousands of dollars were pouring in every hour. On the first day, I made a $40 sale every 43 seconds. By the end of the sale, it had earned $150,000. In just a few days, I earned more than many Americans make in three years.

I was discovering the potential of the internet all over again. While most businesses can only reach a certain percentage of a local population, I could reach the entire world from my laptop. As long as those orange dots kept popping up on the map, and if I could come up with a compelling offer to show those orange dots, I could stay in business. The potential was far more than I had previously imagined.

It's difficult to explain what this success felt like. Just a few weeks prior, I had one of the saddest days in my life when I had to let my employees go and admit that my business was failing. That I was failing. Then, out of the clear blue, I brought in $150,000 in a few days.

The traffic to the website was also growing strong, and more and more people began to know me through my website. In fact, often when I traveled I was recognized in airports and around town. It was really fun that people would stop me and say, "Hey, aren't you Jim Harmer from Improve Photography?" I was just some dude blogging from a laptop, but people around the world began to recognize me. I was soon ranked as one of the top 40 most popular photographers in the world. I'd be lying if I didn't admit it was cool.

Best of all, I had righted the failure story that was developing in my mind before it could finish embedding itself into my life story. Without realizing it, I had allowed my pride to make me start thinking of myself as a successful person. I didn't recognize how dangerous a "success story" can be to one's mental health, happiness, and ability to accept God's will. Success lasts until it doesn't, and you need to remain strong after the success fades.

"I've come through some tough spots in the past and I always make my way through it." The phrase that I at some point heard from an unknown source was now my own story.

The "resiliency story" is the most liberating thing you can tell yourself. When you make a mistake or fail to reach a goal, it no longer throws you into a lengthy introspection about who you are. You're exactly the kind of person who tries really hard and sometimes fails hard anyway. When you see success, you no longer run the risk of forgetting the true source of your blessings. A bout of depression comes, and you take it in stride because you've been through tough stuff before and you always seem to make it through. You end up in a divorce and you know you'll survive.

When working in the last 10% of optimization toward a goal, it can be easy to hit mental limits—upper limits that convince you there's no way to climb higher, or that you are out of place in a position of success.

I also saw the power of weaknesses.

> *None of us like our weaknesses, but I believe we are given our weaknesses for a reason.*

Weaknesses are a gift. Some people stress so much over finding their talent or calling in life. Want to know what your talent is? It's easy. Just think about your weakness. God probably gave that to you so you can grow something strong out of it.

Emily has anxiety and it helps her to be steady and reliable. Because new and unproven things make her anxious, she prefers to keep the status quo sometimes. Her weakness of anxiety helps to make our family happy by keeping us grounded and stable.

With a renewed focus on the core actions that drove 90% of my success, the business continued to grow. The next year, my number one goal was to first reinforce the two parts of my business that were working:

1. driving sales to online courses by consistently publishing content that would bring in new potential customers, and

2. reinforcing the Black Friday flash sale.

The goal was to simply build a moat around what I already had by adding marketing channels to the products and improving the products themselves, rather than going out and starting a *new* social media presence for the company on a new platform or creating a *new* product.

While I spent most of the year working on these goals, I also worked on diversifying the company's income. The opportunity for diversifying was in increasing passive gains on the website. I maintained the publishing schedule of new content that produced 90% of the results in my company and optimized the last 10% by diversifying income streams and marketing.

The Black Friday sale that next year earned $250,000.

How that money changed my family and me is difficult to describe. Emily and I walked around the house for a few weeks constantly remarking to ourselves how insane it was that we earned that much money from a website—from one sale. While we were extremely excited, it was also very painful. This part is difficult to describe unless you've been there. It's what Gay Hendricks in his book *The Big Leap* describes as an "upper-limit problem"—a mental limitation we put on ourselves that can cause distress when we feel we are at a level of success where we don't belong.

The Upper-Limit Problem

Remember the YouTube video about Kony 2012 from several years ago? The video highlighted the plight of the Ugandan people and called for the arrest of the terrorist Joseph Kony by the end of the year 2012. The well-produced humanitarian video attracted over 100 million views—many of them in an extremely short amount of time. The maker of the video was a very decent person who dedicated his time to humanitarian efforts and had a family.

When his project was wildly successful and he finally got attention to the humanitarian issue, he had a mental breakdown almost immediately. A video was recorded of him walking around naked on a screaming tirade in his neighborhood, waving his hands around wildly and soiling himself. This good person who successfully accomplished a good thing had a complete mental breakdown. He later said in an interview with Oprah, "The mind is a powerful thing, and when you feed it with this chaotic noise and everything else, you lose who you are."

Again, I'm not sure I can fully explain what it was like for us to earn a quarter of a million dollars in a week after going through such struggles with the business. It was so sudden that I felt I was losing who I was. I was spending so much time focused on money and work that I could feel myself slipping away. Emily felt the same. We were so stressed and anxious, and yet we felt like we had to double down on work in order to regain control.

We immediately threw ourselves into planning the next flash sale and working on how we would invest the money we'd earned. We started looking at investment properties and deciding which one we should buy. We spent weeks with a real estate agent finding the perfect investment property.

We went to one house with renters in it. The house had an odd odor and a freakishly weird number of mattresses spread around the floors of nearly every room. As we inspected the house, Emily reached for the dishwasher and the guy renting the house flew across the room and physically stopped her from opening it. Weird, we thought. He said there were dirty dishes in there and it was embarrassing. I had a suspicion that there was something illegal in there . . . then we went upstairs and looked through all of the rooms except for one room that had four deadbolts on the door. *Who puts four deadbolts on a bedroom door?* I thought. I looked down and saw six extension cords from other power outlets throughout the house running underneath the door to that room. It was painfully obvious this was a drug house, and it was hilarious seeing the guy living there trying to explain everything. "Oh, this is my brother's room. He's a *very* private person. And he likes to charge his phone on *lots* of different outlets."

We looked at another house being sold significantly under market value because it had been torn apart by renters. There were urine and feces in nearly every room of the house. Something about drugs makes people want to go to the bathroom inside kitchen cabinets, apparently. With the extremely poor condition of the home and what we'd calculated on a total gut of the house, we saw the potential for an extremely good investment. The housing market was still depressed and it was likely we could double our money in just four years.

It was a few weeks before Christmas and Emily and I were driving the kids to a park as we talked about the rental property. Nothing new. The rental property was all we'd talked about for a week. We decided to buy it and that it would be the perfect investment. Property values were at an all-time low and we were in a position to invest. We were well aware of the incredible amount of work it would be and the high costs of the renovation, but the potential for a large profit would be worth it. I called our real estate agent to tell him to place an offer on the house. It was settled. We made a strong offer and would be ready to take possession soon.

I hung up the phone and we drove in silence for about 30 seconds and Emily suddenly said, "This isn't right. I don't feel good about this." I was shocked. We had just spent days talking through every possible scenario and we both thought it was the right course of action. Then 30 seconds of silence pass and suddenly she's against it? Logically, it made little sense, but I knew Emily was close to the Lord and that if she didn't feel right about it, even though she logically thought it was a good idea, then I should trust what she felt.

I called back to the real estate agent right away and told him we didn't want to make the offer after all, and that we decided we weren't going to pursue purchasing a property anymore. The instant I hung up the phone, I felt an overwhelming sense of relief, like we'd dodged a bullet. Trust in that feeling has always led our family to safety. Call it a "gut feeling" or "intuition" or whatever you want; I know it's the voice of one older and wiser than us all.

We didn't buy the rental property, and I'm so grateful for that. I didn't realize at the time how focused on money and work we'd become. We simply shut everything down for a few weeks. No work. No investments. No distractions. We were fully present for Christmas with our two excited little boys who only cared about Santa coming on Christmas morning. Best decision ever.

Money has been a great blessing for our family. It has allowed me to buy our family a fabulous home, go on vacations, and more importantly, to fix so many problems and stressors that come up by simply paying for a solution rather than stressing.

Yet money itself doesn't make us happy. In fact, at some statistical point, money does absolutely nothing to make us happier. The journal *Nature*

Human Behavior published a large study titled "Happiness, income satiation and turning points around the world"[6] of over 1.7 million people, in which they asked about their income level and their satisfaction with their life. The study essentially found that if a person in North America earns between $65,000 and $95,000 per year, they are significantly more likely to have stable emotional well-being than those who earn less. Interestingly though, they found that happiness in life peaked at about the $105,000 per year income level for an individual (more for a household) and that those making more money than that were unlikely to be any happier. The phrase "Money can't buy happiness" is unquestionably true, but it certainly can buy a reduction in stress if spent wisely.

This study confirms what I have experienced. When I was worried about my business's survival and "making it," I was extremely stressed. Then I reached a level where my motivations at work were more about making products for my audience that would delight them, working in the business just for the love of the competition, and enjoying the people I got to work with.

Years ago, a psychologist friend and I were talking around a campfire one evening. I asked him what his favorite question was to ask his patients to understand their problems and how he could help them. He said he started most of his sessions by saying, "Pretend with me that you have gone to sleep for the night, and now have just woken up. When you woke up, you found everything in your life is much better than the day before. What changed to make your life better?" I found the question to be rather intriguing. We talked about it at length and I was surprised to hear that around the campfire, every answer given was something to do with finances. They wished their debt was eliminated, or to win the lottery, or to be able to move to a bigger house, or get a raise at work, etc.

I continued asking that question in conversations for a very long time. I even asked the girl making my Sweet Onion Teriyaki foot-long at Subway one time, and the guy fixing my tires at the mechanic shop. I suspect I have asked that question of nearly 100 people over the years. Only three people have ever given me an answer that wasn't a wish for financial gain. Not health, not relationships, not a stronger spiritual connection to God. No, it's money the world wants.

I could finally understand it. The lack of money can be a major stressor in life and will largely control one's time, yet it doesn't take earning very much more money before a satiation point is reached, and suddenly, more money becomes irrelevant to one's happiness.

One day at a family reunion, someone brought out a time capsule we'd buried five years prior. In it, there was a video message that we'd recorded to ourselves. Here's what we had dreamed of: "We'll probably be in our first house, and it'll probably just be a little one. We'll probably be saving up for a cruise someday. I'll probably be working [as an attorney]." Ha. Our goals weren't anywhere near where we'd ended up.

Yes, my business was successful, but as I looked back on my net worth calculator from the previous years as I tracked my personal finances, I realized there would be no way we could be where we were if we hadn't spent the money we'd earned well. When most people have a high income, they live like it. They get a massive house on a mortgage and buy cars, vacations, and stuff.

Emily and I shared one base model Nissan Sentra for many years. She drove me to work and we crammed three little car seats in the back. We were millionaires before we bought a second car for our family. We lived in a starter home in a starter neighborhood and allowed ourselves just $200 per month each in buying fun stuff. Yes, our income was an amazing blessing for us, but we would have sunk under a pile of debt when the business dipped if we'd lived like most people would when they have a high income that they *think* will last.

Frugality had been a trait that served us very well, but I admit that sometimes we had it to a fault. I had an idea to give my kids a printed "golden ticket" for Christmas that they could redeem for a trip with Dad anywhere in the world. I hesitated and squirmed over whether or not I should do it for about a year. We had plenty of money, but it still just felt unnecessary and overly extravagant—even though it could be a really special experience for my boys to make memories with me one on one. In reality, there was nothing keeping me from doing it. We were saving and completely out of debt and had plenty to make it happen, but I still hesitated for too long.

Eventually, I pulled the trigger. I gave my two little boys a golden ticket. My older son, Ruger, cashed in his ticket for a trip to Japan. My younger son was only four at the time so I didn't think he could handle much of a plane ride so we drove to a city a few hours away for a snowmobiling and skiing adventure in the mountains. At that age, he couldn't really tell the difference between a few hours away and a few countries away, anyway.

Those two trips were perhaps the best two weeks of my life as a parent. Even four years later, I don't think a single week has passed that the kids don't mention something about those trips. Each child felt so special that I spent an entire week just with them individually. Cole and I talk about our snowmobiling adventure in Burgdorf, and Ruger and I talk about the snow monkeys and the terrible food in Japan.

I can hardly believe that I nearly missed those opportunities with my boys because I was pinching my pennies *too* hard and was almost *too* focused on work. I also realized that money should never be an excuse. I had as much fun with my 4-year-old in a city just a couple hours away as I did with my 7-year-old in a country far away. It wasn't the money that made those experiences so special, it was the dedicated one-on-one time. Yet, in planning those trips, all I could focus on was the cost. It was the cost that nearly kept me from that memory.

After those trips were over, I returned to the business and was more motivated than ever to make progress. My goals for the following year were to simply reinforce the income streams of the business by bringing in more customers to the same offerings, improving the conversion rate on the website, and further diversifying the income. In short, I would focus on the simple actions in my business that had brought in 90% of the results and not get distracted by other things.

I did allow myself one side project, however, that I could work on as a way to diversify my income further. My one expansion project for the year was a new website where I would teach online business to others who wanted to create their own website businesses. I originally titled the website ColdFishSticks.com—remembering the experience of eating cold fish sticks in the Florida hotel room with Emily when we were poor. Quickly, however, I realized that was the dumbest possible name for a website, and I changed it.

I spent an entire day trying to find a new domain name for this new website. Finding a good domain name is hard because there are hundreds of millions of websites and most of the good .com domains are taken. I got the idea to title the site "Income School," a site about how to earn an income.

Unfortunately, the domain name "IncomeSchool.com" was already owned by someone else. I looked up his name and contact information by doing a "Who Is" search, and I called him on the phone. He wanted $10,000 for the name, but I was able to negotiate the price down to $2,000. For a short and memorable name like "Income School," I felt it was a bargain.

I decided that on this website I'd share every detail of how I created a site, got website traffic, and then monetized it. I included every detail—with screen recordings of me doing every step so that anyone could learn to do it.

I even created a video course showing every detail of how I made the flash sale that had earned hundreds of thousands of dollars in a single week. I had to laugh when a customer emailed in a complaint that they didn't think the strategy was helpful for them. I had sold this person an exact step-by-step recipe that had earned me hundreds of thousands of dollars in a week by using a unique tactic that I hadn't seen others in the market employing, and yet this guy didn't feel it was worth $50 to learn. Why? Because he saw an incredible result, and immediately his mind told him that he didn't belong there, couldn't do the same thing, and should instead flee from the opportunity.

Humans are lazy lumps of lard when it comes to opportunity. We flee from opportunity and success by nature. We are one of the only living beings capable of making long-term decisions, and even so we aren't particularly good at it. When we stare opportunity in the face, we fear what that new thing may bring into our lives, and we shrink down to the comfortable place we have always been.

I have a mental image I imagine any time I feel myself fleeing from a new opportunity that seems intimidating. It's strange, I'll warn you, but it works for me. I picture an anaconda catching a rabbit. Side note: I have no idea if anacondas even eat rabbits. I picture it coiled up all around the rabbit and ready to squeeze the life out of it. Then it coils its head back, about to plunge its mouth around the rabbit. It stares the rabbit straight in the eyes, and . . . it gets squeamish, loses its appetite, and slinks away. That's what we do when we have opportunities and flee from them. Instead, we need to stare success right in the eyeballs and give the anaconda squeeze. Crush the life out of the opportunity and go in for the kill.

I want to illustrate the importance of my bizarre "anaconda squeeze" analogy with a true story. I had a meeting with a man who was relatively unknown until a few months previous when his book went viral. Almost overnight, he had 300,000 readers talking about his book.

After a chance meeting, I struck up a conversation with him and found out that he was struggling to monetize the audience he had grown, and the book royalties were almost all taken by the publisher. My jaw hit the floor. With an audience of his size and in the niche he was in, he should have been earning six figures per month but he hadn't yet figured out how to capitalize on his idea.

I had worked with online audiences for years and knew exactly how he could create a business around the audience he had grown. I set up a meeting with him and pitched him on a business venture which had virtually no downside for him.

I started the meeting by saying, "Look, today I want to write you a massive check—bigger than you've received in your entire life." You'd think that would make anyone feel ecstatic, right? Nope. I could immediately read the expression on his face, and it wasn't excitement. It was terror. The anaconda lost his stomach for success.

He experienced a lot of success in a short amount of time, and his subconscious was intent on pulling him back down to where he was before the success. He felt, "I don't belong here. This is dangerous. I'm outta here!" He told me he was very interested and excited by the idea and would get back to us in a few days with a decision. As soon as we left the meeting, I told the others that he was going to decline the offer. I knew the anaconda had lost its stomach for further success.

Now that you recognize what an upper-limiting problem is, you'll see it everywhere. Whitney Hansen from *The Money Nerds Podcast* was so excited about her idea for a podcast that she called in sick to work to record 16 episodes in two days. Then? She never released the podcast for over a year because she felt too scared to launch. She had an idea and saw the potential for it, took the first steps and started to taste early success, so her mind fought her to stop and turn back to the safe life she'd lived before. It's a good thing she broke through her upper-limit problem. She now gets 50,000 downloads per month.

Action Step Eight: Go Read *The Big Leap*

No, this isn't an advertisement. No, the author of the book *The Big Leap*, Gay Hendricks, is not my brother-in-law who I'm trying to help out. I've never met him, but honestly, that book is so vitally important at this step of your journey in becoming a goal animal that it's mandatory reading. Go read *The Big Leap* by Gay Hendricks.[7] What we just discussed in this chapter about reaching an upper limit to your success and backing down from opportunity is exactly what the entire book is all about. My ability to reach higher goals has significantly increased after reading that book.

Anyway, I was telling you about the book *The Big Leap* by Gay Hendricks. It was as if the author had seen deep into my soul and helped me see things I had no idea were there. In the book, Hendricks describes what he calls the "upper-limit problem" and how one of the things that keeps us from transcending is that we are stuck doing work that is not within our "zone of genius."

The upper-limit problem means that we achieve some level of success, and we immediately work to bring ourselves back down to mediocrity. We feel uncomfortable being super-performers because we have told ourselves so many negative things about ourselves that it doesn't feel like who we really are.

At first when I began listening to the book, I didn't realize I was allowing myself to frequently hit an upper limit of happiness and success before coming back down to mediocrity. Yet now I notice myself doing it on an almost weekly basis. Before I took my family on an amazing vacation, I found myself stressed to the max with my websites and working from early morning to late at night.

My wife asked me what I was so worried about. I told her there was a dip in traffic on one of my sites and I wasn't sure what was causing it. She asked me if it was normal to see a very temporary dip in traffic like this. I realized it was. Yes, it's perfectly normal to see fluctuations if one of the articles hasn't been shared around on social media lately or if it's the holiday season when fewer people are searching online. Suddenly, I realized there was no actual problem. The week prior was Christmas. There is always a dip in traffic the week of Christmas, and I knew that perfectly well. The issue was not that I couldn't figure out the problem. What was actually happening was that I just had a wonderful Christmas season with my family. I had hardly checked on work at all for weeks. We were just about to go on an amazing vacation with the kids. The problem was that I had hit an upper limit of happiness and success. I felt out of control because I felt like I should be worried about something or working hard on some insurmountable problem, or else this happiness and success would go away. I had an upper-limit problem.

I even feel this problem creeping into my life right now. While I have worked on this book for years, now that the January 1 publishing date grows closer, I feel myself wanting to hold back and not open myself up for criticism. I find myself saying, "People are going to rip this book to shreds in their reviews. It won't matter that I talk about so many of my failings and weaknesses. They'll just focus on the fact that I talk about achieving my goals and they'll say I'm self-centered and conceited." That may be true, but I think the actual fear is upper-limiting.

You have analyzed your work energy, decided on what you need to work on and what actions will get you there, and you're seeing your first bricks stacked up behind your house. Now is when the problems start. In the last chapter, you learned how to avoid good ideas at this point, and now you are going to read *The Big Leap* and learn how to not upper-limit yourself.

9

THE GHOST TOWN

"Doubt kills more dreams than failure ever will."
—Suzy Kassem

With my main site stabilized and a new small team working to help me maintain the 90% actions in the business, I felt ready to slowly expand my business again. I had learned so much from my mistakes that I wanted to start over from scratch, so I decided to grow a second site.

I would apply the same work energy formula to my work on this second site. Essentially, I would pick a topic for the site and focus only on creating one new piece of content each day—the 90% action. Along the way, I'd feed my work energy by waking up each morning and looking at my stats of traffic from the site. Nothing motivates me like looking at those orange dots on the map showing people around the world visiting my sites. "Look at me, Ma! People are coming to my website!" Then, after I achieved solid traffic to the site by groundhogging the 90% action, I would continue those actions as I began to optimize the business for further monetization.

One day I was looking over websites for sale when I found a listing for a survival site. The site was earning a couple thousand dollars per month, but had strong traffic. I bought it for $32,000. After the purchase, I immediately changed the organization and design of the site to one I knew from experience would do better. Within a matter of weeks, the site traffic and income spiked. I hired a teenager to write a few more articles on the site, but eventually that stopped as well. I simply left the site and did not do any further writing on it for a few years. I had never left a site like this and thought the traffic would go down quickly, but I was wrong.

Actually, the rankings on search engines were consistent for many years, even when I added no new content. The site grew to earn over $5,000 per month consistently and I eventually sold it for $184,000. With the purchase price and the money I'd earned on the site for the years I'd owned it, I made 15 times my original $32,000 investment.

Building From Scratch

It was time for another website, and again I applied the same work energy formula for accomplishing the goal. This time the topic was boats. For many months, I'd saved money and eyed boats. I am not from a boating family and had never water-skied in my life, but who wouldn't love the wind in their hair as they magically walked on the water? I spent many hours researching boats and finally settled on a gorgeous new 32-foot pontoon boat with a 150hp engine. I drove to the dealership and wrote a check for the boat. The salesman asked me if I wanted any help hooking it up to my truck when I suddenly realized I didn't even own a truck, and I'd just bought a very large and very heavy boat. Not kidding. That's how well planned this was. I've always been more of a "ready, fire, aim" type of person. I sold one of our vehicles and traded for a truck the next day so I could drive my purchase home.

I had saved up and paid cash for the boat, and it was well within our means, but I still felt sick about spending that much money on a boat. As I drove it home with my new truck, I looked in the rearview mirror and I swear it sneered at me with a look that said, "You're such a sucker. You've wasted your money on me and you're gonna go broke some day and regret ever having bought me." Remember the upper limit problem? It was rearing its ugly head. The day I put my boat into the lake for the first time, I bought a new .com domain where I'd share everything I'd learned about boating during my months of research. My goal was to earn as much from this blog as I'd spent on my boat—in effect making my boat free.

I looked back on my Google search history for all of the searches I'd made about boats as I researched my purchase, and then I wrote on my blog the answers that I'd learned. I was not a boating expert by any means—just an amateur sharing his newly gained insights.

I had many self-doubts as I worked on this site. Yes, I had built one successful site and flipped another site, but this was only my second time building a site from scratch. I wasn't sure if I could figure out how to get the traffic, or if people would like reading a blog from a newbie's perspective. Many times I wondered if I was just wasting my time.

I designed a day to achieve my goal. I would simply wake up each morning and before I was allowed to do any other work on my main site, I would spend 90 minutes writing a new blog post on the boating website. I wrote 35 articles over the course of six weeks and left the site to organically grow on search.

It generally takes Google about eight months to show articles from a new website high enough on its search engine rankings that people will find them, so nothing was really happening on this new site. I've come to refer to this phase of working on a goal as the "ghost town" phase, because it feels like you are the only person in a ghost town. You can go into the town square and shout as loud as you want, yet no crowd gathers. "Um . . . hello? Is anyone here? I made a blog. Wanna come see it?" That's kind of what it's like to start a new business or achieve any goal. No one notices your work for a long time.

One of the most difficult mental barricades to achieving a goal is pushing through the ghost town phase. No one can see a physical difference in you after you've only been running for a week. No one loves your paintings after only a few lessons. No one recognizes you as a good basketball player after you go shoot hoops three times in a week. The ghost town is the phase where you are left alone with hard work, little perceived progress, and no indicators of what those continued 90% actions could eventually help you achieve.

About a year later, I checked back on the boating website to find it booming. Those 35 articles were bringing in over 30,000 pageviews per month, and the site earned as much as $4,000 per month. My focused 90% actions had worked. They simply needed time to rank well on search engines.

I had spent only a few weeks writing the 35 articles on the boating website, and it was bringing in thousands of dollars per month now. The site earned money from Amazon's affiliate program. I mentioned boating products that I liked, and people who read my articles would sometimes click on my link to Amazon to buy the product. When they did, I would get about 4% of the sale. Anyone can sign up for Amazon's affiliate program, and anyone can start a blog to drive traffic there.

Our family really enjoyed our "free" boat. We spent many summer days motoring around the deep-green mirror reflections of Anderson Ranch Reservoir. Emily and the kids also spent many days freezing their buns off while I fished for Kokanee salmon early and late in the season. We eventually decided that the warm boating season in Idaho was simply too short, and we sold the boat to trade it for an RV.

I sold the boating site for $74,000. Given the sale price and what the site had earned to that point, I earned three times more from the blog than I'd spent on that beautiful boat.

> *If my love for internet business hasn't come through yet, I'll just make it clear right here: I am in love with my work.*

We bought a new Harmer Family Camping Machine with the purchase of a great travel trailer from the money we'd received from selling the boat. Although we didn't spend any extra money, I still hated writing the check to buy our camper. So, I registered a new site—CamperReport.com.

As I began this new blog, I became very intentional about my approach to writing the content. I had learned a tremendous amount about how to get traffic to a website quickly, and I decided to create a formalized, step-by-step process for building these passive income websites to ensure I was only focusing on the actions that drove 90% of the result at first. I took what I'd learned from the boating site and laid out a plan to create this new site in less than two months and eventually have the site earn several thousand dollars a month.

The ghost town phase of a goal is only difficult for those who haven't spent time there before. Yes, it was still difficult for me to write blog posts to thin air. No one was reading my blog posts when I started, and sometimes I would doubt that it would work again, but since I had now already successfully built three online businesses, it became easier.

For someone who has never seen their abdominal muscles in their entire life, it can be difficult to believe they are even in there. For someone who has never seen an A on a paper, it can be difficult to believe you could ever finish college. For someone like me, who can't cook anything other than cereal and toast, it can be difficult to believe you could become a great chef.

I created the content for Camper Report over a period of about 60 days. I wrote 35 articles—the same as I'd done on the boating site. This time, however, I learned that I could tweak the order in which I wrote the posts to bring in traffic more quickly. I wrote shorter posts on more niche topics at first so they could rank for keywords with almost no competition on Google. Later, I focused on keywords that received more searches and were more sought after by other bloggers with larger sites.

Camper Report grew significantly faster than the boating site with this tweak to the recipe. I worked to formulate the perfect recipe for creating sites in a short period of time that could earn passive income. I also added a YouTube channel to Camper Report to push people to the blog. I only recorded 10 videos, but some of those videos received hundreds of thousands of views and really launched the site quickly.

Now that Camper Report has had time to grow organically on search engine rankings, it gets over 300,000 pageviews per month and brings in about $10,000 per month. That's incredible, considering the very small amount of time that was invested to get the site up and running initially.

Not only was my portfolio of new websites growing, but I was able to maintain them well by growing a small team to help me. I had created a rinse-and-repeat formula for creating successful online businesses on YouTube and in blogs.

I felt compelled to share with other people how they could provide for their families by creating online businesses. I had worked with so many friends over the years who gave up on themselves during the ghost town phase of creating online businesses, and it discouraged me that no one was taking advantage of what could be done.

I can't count the number of times I stayed up late sitting at the dining room table with friends who were struggling financially—explaining to them everything I'd learned about internet marketing and how they could create a business of their own.

No matter how excited they were at our first meeting, and no matter how many times they assured me they were going to be the one who would actually follow through, they all ended up quitting. A decent website needs a significant initial batch of content on it before it can be left to passively grow. Too small of a website won't give Google enough reason to pay attention to it because it will have fewer lines in the water gathering traffic and links to the site. I saw dozens of people write 5 or 10 articles and then they let the ghost town phase kill their project. If only they could have believed in themselves—they were so very close to success.

I decided to share the process I'd created online. I registered a new website where I would share my recipe—IncomeSchool.com. I created the site and did what I had always done. I wrote an article a day, answering the questions I had asked when I first started blogging. The site grew to modest success with a few thousand in earnings, but it wasn't big enough to get excited about yet. I didn't want to abandon the site, but I needed to focus my attention elsewhere in my business.

Emily and I spent many hours talking about what to do. My time was undoubtedly better spent by simply working on my other sites, in terms of ROI, but I felt compelled to work on Income School and build it up to help other people.

I can't remember how, but the name of someone who could help popped into my head. Ricky Kesler. Ricky was my best friend in high school. We had chased the same girls, played the same sports, and basically spent every second together for four years. We even worked the same part-time job at a musical instrument repair shop where, on your first day, one of the women who owned the shop would body-slam a tuba onto the cement and ask you to fix it, in order to teach you the trade.

Ricky was an MBA student at a top school at the time, which I thought would be a good fit for the subject matter of the site—teaching people how to start an internet business. We had connected sporadically since high school but life was busy and we hadn't kept up. When we both lived in different cities in Brazil for two years as full-time missionaries, I once mailed him a dead cockroach as a joke. Oh, and during the height of the anthrax scare, I mailed him a few tablespoons of wheat flour. Other than that, we didn't have much contact. Yet, as soon as I thought of him I knew he was the person I should be working with on Income School. He has always been smart as a whip and someone with whom I got along very well. I guess once you've fixed a body-slammed tuba together and mailed dead cockroaches to each other, you're bonded for life.

I called Ricky and spent some time catching up, and then told him about the spot I was in. I had a site that was growing slowly but had enough traction that it shouldn't be ignored and left to die. He was immediately on board and began writing on the site. We created Income School LLC and split the baby 50/50.

Our blog posts on internet marketing weren't performing well on Google because the topic was very competitive, so we decided to create a podcast. Week after week, we recorded episodes and desperately tried to grow an audience, but the show never grew past a few thousand downloads per episode. We were feeling discouraged in the ghost town phase of the site. We just couldn't make the business grow.

Next, we tried making a YouTube channel. Week after week, it proved to be the same battle as we had with the podcast. We just couldn't get enough traction to grow the site.

We became frustrated with trying to teach people our recipe for building online businesses, so we eventually decided to just make our own websites as had worked in the past. We decided we'd sell Income School, which was earning a few thousand per month, but not enough to get us excited about it.

We went through weeks of paperwork and then called our business broker to help us sell the site. I was at a family reunion at the time, so we had a three-way call as I stepped onto the deck of the cabin where we were staying. Because of a technicality in the way the site's valuation was done, we wouldn't get as much for the business as we'd hoped. Right there on the call, Ricky and I decided we would walk away from the deal and continue to build Income School.

As soon as I hung up the phone, I had an overwhelming feeling that I had just dodged a bullet. I knew the thought came from one much older and wiser than any of us in the world, because it brought with it a knowledge I didn't have. I knew right then that Income School would eventually become something very important to me. Selling it would have been disastrous.

I had built up a handful of businesses from scratch at this point, but still, the ghost town phase of building this new site was crushing. One day I'd feel like we had it in the bag, and the next day I'd feel like we'd never succeed and that we were wasting our time in a market that was too competitive. Trudging through the ghost town phase is by far the hardest barricade to achieving anything.

> *Without question, the number one reason people fail in internet marketing is because they quit during the ghost town phase and don't give the project enough time to succeed.*

What goals have you given up on, just days before you would have seen enough success to convince you to continue on?

Our YouTube channel seemed to be the answer. We began seeing sales of our online course trickle in, and in the customer survey we saw more and more people saying they found us through our tiny YouTube channel.

New Groundhog Day

We saw YouTube as a way to break through the ghost-town phase on this difficult project, so we changed the groundhog day we had designed. We stopped writing articles, and we designed a day to help us produce YouTube videos consistently, and we groundhogged it.

We finally found the right 90% action to groundhog. The business immediately began to grow.

We also built other sites during this time to refine our recipe for creating an online business. I bought a 50cc dirt bike for my boys and our family was instantly hooked. Nothing stokes a father's pride quite like seeing his son in dirt biking pads, revving up an engine. If I were Tim Allen, I'd let out a manly grunt right here.

Since we had many sites following our other hobbies, we created DirtBikePlanet.com and built that site to nearly 100,000 pageviews per month and strong earnings. Now, pushing through the ghost town phase of a new site wasn't at all intimidating since we had been through it so many times before.

Eventually, we took everything we learned and put it into a step-by-step process. Sixty steps to creating passive income online. We called the online course Project 24 because people in the course would have a goal of replacing their current income with money from passive income websites in 24 months. The course has been a massive success with thousands of customers from all around the world.

Most people who get stuck in the ghost town phase of any goal are stuck there because they have failed in other things in the past. Our minds seem to keep score, and if you've failed in many things in a row, some people become convinced that they are the ones who cannot succeed.

However cursed you feel, however many times you've come up short, however many weaknesses you seem to have that others do not, the truth is there is no scoreboard that fixes your chances the next time you attempt something great. The truth is that when you take on your next project, you are no more likely or less likely to succeed because of the failures of your past.

The only thing that can keep you from getting what you want is the belief that you somehow are destined to fail.

Why do so many people stay in debt their entire adult lives? Because it's difficult to get excited about skipping a restaurant to save $10 when you have $60,000 in debt. Why do so few people develop a strong relationship with God? Because initially, repentance and change is hard and the rewards of peace and happiness don't come until after the hard change. It is the ghost town that keeps us from accomplishing the things we most want out of life.

There are essentially three reasons why we quit during the ghost town phase:

1. A belief that we will not achieve the goal despite the work
2. A belief that we don't belong in that level of achievement as discussed earlier in the book about the anaconda squeeze
3. A belief that the goal is ultimately not worth the effort

Everything you have ever started and not finished likely traces back to one of those three reasons. The work energy formula has been designed specifically to combat those three things.

The first belief that you will not achieve the goal despite the work can pop up in many ways. As the mayor of your "ghost town of a goal," you make many efforts to improve the town but see no one moving in, so you quit. You lose a few pounds but then go three weeks in a row without losing a pound, so you quit. The work energy formula combats this problem by *identifying only the most essential actions to achieve 90% of the result* so that your actions are most directly tied to results, which makes you confident that your approach will reach the goal.

The last belief that the goal is ultimately not worth the effort is another common issue we run into because we are lazy lumps of lard. We see success in dieting until there's an opportunity to eat out with friends and we weigh the benefit of staying on the diet versus going out with friends. Often, we make short-term decisions and say the goal is not worth it. We convince ourselves it is okay to ruin the plot of our groundhogging because *today*, more happiness would be won by going out to dinner with friends. Yet we all know that in the long run that dinner will be worth little, but achieving your goal could change the course of your life.

When in the ghost town phase, never allow short-term thinking to stop your progress.

Action Step Nine: Identify the Beliefs Your Mind Will Use Against You

All of your objections in the ghost town phase can be categorized into three groups:

1. A belief that you will not achieve the goal despite your work
2. A belief that you don't belong in that level of achievement
3. A belief that the goal is ultimately not worth the effort

Think through the beliefs in each of those categories and seek to understand how your mind will use them against you. That way, when you're invited to dinner to break your diet, or you are tired and don't want to study Spanish one evening, or you are trying to get out of debt but you want to go to Playa Del Carmen, you'll have a plan and understand how your goal fits into the bigger picture.

10

TO ALL THOSE WHO HAVE WRITTEN FAILURE STORIES WITHIN THEMSELVES

"Success is an ugly thing. Men are deceived by its false resemblances to merit . . . They confound the brilliance of the firmament with the star-shaped footprints of a duck in the mud."
—Victor Hugo, Les Misérables

Earlier, I discussed not allowing a success story to write itself into your life. If you think of yourself as defined by your successes in business, sports, or anything else, your sense of identity will be lost, should your life change. I also shared a time when I came very close to allowing a failure to etch itself into my story, which would have been difficult to remove. Remember your new story: "I've taken some tough hits and lived through some worrisome situations, but somehow I always end up on top."

You may not see yourself that way. At some point along the way, you have allowed yourself to write a failure story. You understand the steps in this book and how following them could lead you to achieve greater heights than ever before, but somewhere within you there's a feeling of "But that's not me. I don't finish the things I start. I want to do great things, but I tend to flame out right as I reach mediocrity." You're an underdog.

This chapter is only for you. There are some people I love who feel as you do, and so I feel that I understand you. I wish I could sit down with you, knee to knee, and talk with you about where you've been and where you want to go. I'm rooting for you and I can show you that change is closer than your story will allow you to see right now.

First, let's talk about where you have been, and where I've been. Several years ago, I went on a photography trip to Ireland. Given that my business was entirely online and monetized through other means, I thought it would be a unique marketing tool to hold free, in-person photography trips in many different photogenic locations around the world. Most well-known photographers charged thousands of dollars for these trips, so I thought it might attract attention if I periodically held free workshops around the world. This one was in Ireland and a small group of people who followed me online joined me for the trip.

As I looked for photo locations to shoot, the Dark Hedges kept popping up in my searches. The Dark Hedges are a group of trees lining a long, straight road leading up a hill. The trees are over 250 years old, and their limbs climb upward in contorted, wavy stretches.

The Dark Hedges are a famous landmark. They have been photographed millions of times by tourists from around the world, and I'm told they appear in famous TV shows like Game of Thrones. I wanted to do something different. I wanted to stretch myself creatively and take a photo there that stood out from the rest.

The photo I wanted to take was of a woman with a flaming torch wearing a dress befitting an older period of time where castles, kings, and queens ruled the land, standing in the middle of the old road leading through the Dark Hedges. Along with those with me on the trip, we began planning. We found a great model who could travel to the location with us for the shoot. We found the perfect dress and researched how to make a flaming torch on YouTube.

Planning the shoot with the other photographers who lived in Europe was much more difficult than I imagined. I told them about my vision for the shoot multiple times, and they just couldn't get excited about it. I kept telling them that a model in old clothes with a torch would be perfect, but they didn't seem to like the idea. Finally, during one of our brainstorming sessions, I said, "You guys, we just *have* to do the shot of the model with the flaming torch." There was an awkward silence for a minute and then they all started laughing when they realized what I meant. Apparently in Europe, a torch is what Americans would call a flashlight. They thought I wanted our model in period clothing to be holding a Maglite up to her face.

Finally, the day of the shoot came, and we began with about an hour of prep work. After hair and makeup, and working through posing, we were only waiting for the perfect lighting. The flame on the torch was drowned out by the natural light, and I wanted her face to be partially lit by the warm yellow light of the torch. We waited for what photographers call an equalization point, when the brightness of the ambient light matches the artificial light source of the torch.

Several buses full of tourists came to the rural location while we were there, and just as the last bus left, we began the shoot. The first few minutes went well and I got some shots I was starting to be happy with, but the torch had begun to flame out.

We were trying to hurry while the light was right, so one of the people on the trip with me took the torch from the young model and brought over a can of gasoline to add flame to the torch. In a momentary lapse of thinking, he poured gas from the can straight onto the already-lit flame on the previously gas-soaked cloth on the stick. Immediately, the fire leapt up the stream of gasoline and shot straight into the can. The entire can burst into a flame right in his hands.

If he had any time to think, he could have simply let go of the can and set it down on the pavement to let it safely burn out, but in a second momentary lapse of judgment, he flung the can somewhere unimaginable—into a thick pile of knee-high weeds beside the road. Yes, the road where the world-famous trees were.

I could see the headlines. I was responsible for a forest fire that burned down a national treasure, and was going to spend years in an Irish prison being beat to a pulp by Conor McGregor. What a turn of events from only seconds before! My blood ran cold as the gravity of what had just happened sank in.

The gas can landed upside down and a large flaming ball of gas gurgled out immediately when the can hit the ground. The fiery gasoline began running down the hill on the edge of the road. In a matter of seconds, the raging flame spanned 20 feet along the embankment.

Everyone sprang into action. We poured out every water bottle on the flame, which seemed to drink the water without quenching its thirst. In fact, the water seemed to make it worse, as it mixed with the liquid of the gas and further spread it out. If you have ever seen a gasoline fire, you know the flame simply cannot be stopped like a simple wood fire. I positioned myself at the end of the flame to prevent it from spreading, and began stomping furiously on the flame to put it out. As soon as my boot lifted from a spot, the flame returned immediately. The gasoline burned so hot and long that there was nothing I could do to end the burning.

I trenched out an area with my boot in the dirt to keep all other weeds away, and ran madly back and forth along the flames until they caught the bottom of my pants on fire and began melting the rubber bottoms of my Merrell boots.

Passersby stopped at the sight and one of the people on the trip went over to them and told them we were filming a scene for Game of Thrones and had the situation under control. I couldn't imagine how he could even think of a joke at that moment.

The fire burned and burned and nothing seemed to slow it from finishing out what it had begun. Yet, after unimaginably long minutes battling the flames, we began to make progress. The fire was dying down. Fortunately, it had rained just a few hours earlier and as the gasoline burned out, I was shocked to see that the weeds did not even appear to be singed. I could not believe it. Fifteen minutes earlier I was fairly sure I would spend a significant portion of my adult life in an Irish prison, and now it looked as if nothing had ever happened.

We remained at the scene for over an hour after the final flame went out to be absolutely certain the fire was completely and entirely stopped. We cleaned up the area perfectly so that not even any burned grass remained to tell the tale. It looked as if nothing had happened. Somehow, that raging fire disappeared with the gasoline, and the wet grass never caught. We were incredibly fortunate that we'd set up our model in a spot between the trees and the fire was never closer than 40 feet from a tree. The group left, but we assigned two people in our group to remain there for an additional two hours to further assure that not a single ember could possibly still have been hot.

I didn't calm down for a week. I could barely breathe for days. I can't express how relieved I was to get on an airplane headed home from Ireland.

There's a point to sharing the most frightening moment of my life. Here it is: Please tell me just one time—ever—in your entire life, when you worried and stewed over something and it actually turned out as bad or worse than you had imagined. Okay—it may only have happened once or twice that you worried about something that actually was worth worrying about. Even then, worrying didn't help solve the problem.

How many nights as a teenager did you worry over a test the next day? Do you remember getting stomachaches as you stressed about math class the next day? Given time and life experience, you undoubtedly can now see how unnecessary that fear was. The test that felt so monumentally vital to you at the time isn't even notable in your life's story today.

Yes, you may have stressed and worried about a crumbling marriage and in the end it was actually horrible. You weren't able to save the marriage and suffered a crushing divorce. Yet here you are. Remember? "You've lived through some tough stuff, and somehow you always make it through."

Yes, you may have stressed and worried about your job and in the end you did actually get laid off or fired. Yet here you are. Maybe you've found better work and an improved financial situation, or you soon will.

You almost certainly have written a failure story that is not accurate. We always see things far worse than they actually are, and the successes that eluded you were likely so close to your grasp that it was by an inch that you missed them. Yes, the result of a divorce, bankruptcy, heart attack, or other catastrophic failure may have changed your life; however, the action that caused those failures was likely extremely minor. It was a few poor choices at key moments. You actually weren't miles away from success; you were so close you could taste it, but one or two small things kept it from you.

The point is that success and failure swing on a tight hinge. If it hadn't rained an hour before that photo shoot, things may have ended as badly as I imagined. If you hadn't done that one marketing campaign, your business may have dried up and you may have needed to close your doors. If, that one time, you had decided to give in to weakness and smoked that cigarette, you may still be addicted today. If you had gone on just one more day flirting with that woman or man at work, it could have led to the destruction of your marriage.

Most of our successes come not from heroic efforts of raw willpower and self-discipline for prolonged periods, but are determined by very simple choices at critical moments. The same can be said of our failures, which usually are the result of a few key missteps that cause you to narrowly miss your goal. If you feel there is a failure story written in your soul, rest assured the failure was likely because of something so easily preventable that you will have no trouble changing your story going forward.

Building a Goal Muscle

We see people achieving incredible things each day, thanks to the ease of our communication. Our phones are only a few taps away from showing us the best-looking people on the planet through Instagram, the most gorgeous homes through Pinterest, the most genius business decisions through podcast interviews, the most incredible music through Spotify, and your neighbor down the street who goes on exotic vacations with his model wife every two weeks through Facebook.

The message I keep hearing is that social media is dangerous to our mental health, and I 100% agree. Yet a small change to our attitudes can yield an entirely different result. What if we began to see the path to all incredible successes as beginning with a very small success?

There is a neighborhood my wife and I have always enjoyed driving through. The houses are massive modern castles of 10,000-plus square feet, with beautifully manicured lawns and a perfect location near Boise, Idaho. Every time I drive through that neighborhood, I feel inspired. I don't feel even slightly jealous or beat down. Quite the opposite, I take inspiration from seeing the heights people have achieved. Yet I think most people would not feel that way. The reason it builds me up when that may tear others down is because I have a 100% belief that I can achieve any level of financial success I want. I have already gone from literally owning nothing that couldn't fit in a single suitcase to becoming a multimillionaire.

It actually feels like a relief to see people ahead of me so I know what's possible. It's exciting.

People who have written a failure story have a difficult time feeling that way. They may momentarily, but in the long run they feel beaten down by the success of others.

Here's why: Most of the goals you make are the goals you've also seen other people achieve. You see people saying they have a goal of losing 20 pounds, so when it's time for you to make a goal, you select 20 pounds. You see people wanting to be totally debt-free, so that's the goal you choose. You see people wanting to be successful entrepreneurs, so that's the goal you set.

Those people can set those goals because they have built a muscle for achieving goals. You have not yet built that muscle. Not yet. Right now, you're an underdog. That's the secret to why you try and fail and fail and fail. That's why success always seems just outside your grasp. All that frustration, all those worries, all that hopelessness and feeling like you could simply never measure up, and now you know why. You've been trying to bench-press 300 pounds without ever bench-pressing 100 pounds.

Some people are goal animals. I have my failures too, but sometimes I can be one of those goal animals. I decided I wanted to break a world record in something, so I just picked up and did it one day. I flipped through a world record book and found the longest distance anyone has ever traveled while shooting tiddlywinks. You remember tiddlywinks. It's the game your grandma played where you have two plastic coins. One lies on the ground and the other in your hand. You pinch the wink on the ground with the plastic coin in your hand and it makes the one on the ground hop forward a few inches. I did it for 2.5 miles and broke the world record. Then I broke a record again by making the most light orbs ever captured in a single photograph. I'm a goal animal. I love it. When I see something I want to do, I just go do it.

You're going to become a goal animal over the course of the next few weeks, but your goals won't be breaking dumb records just for the sake of doing so. You'll build a goal-achieving muscle that you can use to help you crush any goal in your path.

For now, however, you wonder why you can't seem to achieve anything. You can't follow through on your easy goal to read the Bible cover-to-cover this year, or even to just once be the one picked for the promotion or to be in the spotlight. Just once.

Don't make goals like goal animals do. Make underdog goals. That's how you build your goal muscle. I'll show you exactly how to do it in the action step.

Action Step Ten: Set an Underdog Goal and Achieve It

Over the next few weeks, I want you to set simple goals that will not be accomplished without effort, but which will train you to expect a result from your work.

Here are a few examples.

Save $40 by not wasting money on stupid stuff during the week. Each time you don't spend on something that you normally would, you open up the notes app on your phone and write it down as a credit into your imaginary account. Then go out on Saturday and buy something frivolous that you'd like.

If the spark of enjoyment and trust between you and your significant other isn't what it once was, set a goal to do something about it this week. Call him or her on the phone right now—even if you are in the same house already—and ask for a date on Saturday night. Actually perform work to make a change this week. Pick up a nice new dress or dress shirt and lay it on the bed the morning of the date with a note letting them know you think they'd look great in it. Recreate your first date or go somewhere you normally wouldn't. When you have five free minutes during the week, Google some deep conversation starters and open the notes app on your phone to write down the questions you'd like to ask during dinner. Allow yourself to see that you can put work into something and see an actual, tangible result from it in a short period of time.

Lose two pounds in the next seven days. No, this isn't a starting place for losing more. Don't think about the future. Just two pounds. Just lose two pounds. Just prove to yourself that you can make the number on the scale do whatever you tell it to do. Losing two pounds in a week isn't hard, but it will not happen unless you choose to work on it. So you'll grow a goal muscle that trains your mind to expect a result from work.

Set a goal to learn only four chords on the guitar. Only four. Those are the only four chords you need to know to play "Time of Your Life" on the guitar. The purpose is not to give you a starting place for learning the guitar. The goal is to play the song, and to do so you simply need to memorize four chords. It will take a few hours this week, but at the end of the week you will have an ability that you currently don't. You'll see a tangible result.

It is important that you do not view these goals as stepping-stones. These goals do not have value for what they could become if you did them on a grander scale. This goal has more value than anything else because the purpose is to change *you*. You will become a different person by developing the goal muscle. In biblical terms, your goal muscle is simply called faith, and you can move mountains with it when you become the kind of person that God can trust with His miracles. Develop your goal muscle.

Rachel Hollis, in her excellent book *Girl, Wash Your Face,* calls this "keeping a promise to yourself." We are dependable to everyone else in our lives, but when we need to keep a promise to ourselves (such as sticking with a goal today), we lie to ourselves and let ourselves down. We aren't dependable to ourselves, and so we consistently fail.

You're going to be a goal animal! Just doing this simple exercise of making a tiny goal where you can see a tangible result in one week and actually doing it can completely change your life. Soon enough, the rock-solid abs on your friend in her Facebook photo won't tear you down—it'll inspire you. It won't feel out of reach. It'll feel exciting to see what can be done and you'll know you can have it any time you want it. The only reason seeing others succeed is hard is because you believe you can't have it. Building your goal muscle is how you change that belief.

Make your underdog goal.

11

THE PURPOSE OF OUR DREAMS

> *"The new year lies before you like a spotless tract of snow; be careful how you tread, for every mark will show."*
> *—Author unknown*

I hate this chapter. I am well aware of the fact that mentioning right up front that even the author doesn't like the chapter is not a smart way to grab readers' attention, but I already messed up the foreword and dedication, so I think by now you know that I'm kind of a mess.

It's the truth, though. I hate this chapter. I've written it, read it, rewritten it, deleted it four different times, and cried over my keyboard nearly every time. Yes, me. A grown man in tears over his own writing. I don't want to talk about this at all, but I believe part of my life happened for a reason that many people could learn from, so I feel obligated to share it.

This chapter of the story starts earlier in my life—much earlier. I have five older brothers. I'm the youngest. Like every youngest brother, one of your older brothers is always your hero. Mine was Sam.

Sam was on the football team. All the girls wanted him. He was popular because of his peculiar talent to bring a level of fun and enthusiasm to anything he did, unlike anyone else I've ever met. Creativity and excitement radiated out of him and people ate it up. He used that talent for good and befriended people from every walk of life.

He once made a 10-foot-tall T-rex, suspended in the tall entryway of our family home. It was made entirely of toilet paper rolls, which he spent a year saving. He thought it was a great idea to take our old Ford minivan four-wheeling, and got it high-centered on a rock. He sneaked into the house and begged me and another brother to help him push it out of the canyon so my parents wouldn't know. He lined his truck bed with plastic and spent all afternoon boiling pots of water to put in it so he could create a mobile hot tub in the bed of his truck.

When Sam was a teenager, one of the girls in the neighborhood, who was about to turn 16, confided in him that she felt lonely and that people didn't like her. When Sam found out, he got all of the teenage boys in the neighborhood to dress up in suits and ties and individually deliver a rose to her at her front door. He didn't want anything from her. He wasn't trying to date her. He just wanted her to feel good about herself, and he wasn't afraid of going to great lengths to achieve it.

My memories of growing up center mostly around things I did with Sam—despite being several years younger. We played Ninja Turtles in the backyard, hunted invisible enemy insurgents through the mangroves near our home on the beach in Fort Kam, Hawaii, and threw the football in the backyard for uncountable hours. Yet it was playing catch with a baseball that I remember the most. He wanted to be the pitcher, so I'd play catcher, and on more than a few occasions I remember catching his fastball until my fingers literally started bleeding. I didn't want to let on that I was in pain because then he'd stop playing with me.

Sam was the best I've ever met at implementing the principles in this book. From a very young age, he was eager to take things on and he worked constantly to improve at everything he did. As his skills at so many things improved, he felt no fear to take on bigger and tougher challenges. When he played the piano at church, he wasn't afraid to mix a Billy Joel song in the bass line. A normal person would be afraid that people would notice his subtle joke, or that trying to pull it off would make him stumble in front of everyone. Not him. He'd go for it.

A normal college professor would simply teach a lesson. Sam harnessed the talents of his PR students into taking on massive service projects to bring awareness to charities, and he invited many of his students to lunch at his home with his family so he could mentor them. A normal person would not put things on his bucket list like "Get in a bar fight" or "Stow away on a train." Sam grew enough confidence that he didn't have to play the small game anymore. If it seemed interesting, he would go after it without fear.

We grew up, and life began to happen. His body wasn't perfect, as medical depression hit him in his thirties. His marriage fell apart and he was separated from his wife. It was the Fourth of July. Early in the morning, Sam took off on his Harley, unable to bear the day. At lunchtime, I was busy building a treehouse in the backyard with my boys.

At that same moment, in a city only two hours away, my dear brother was driving around town to find a tattoo parlor. Evil Knievel was famous for jumping the canyon in Twin Falls, and Sam thought it'd be hilarious if, when people found his dead body, he had an Evil Knievel tattoo on his forehead. He was in the deepest depression and could not think straight. My brother was planning his end.

He wouldn't answer his phone all day, but I got a text from him. "I'm sorry for not being a better brother. I love you."

Around 9 p.m., Sam drove his motorcycle to the parking lot, walked to the middle of the I.B. Perrine Bridge in Twin Falls and stared at death 486 meters below. He stripped naked and stood up on the railing.

The phone rang and we all knew something was very wrong. A family member answered: "Are you Sam Harmer's brother? He committed suicide in Twin Falls." It was over. Then, another minute later, a second call. He had *attempted* suicide. All of us wondered what that meant, exactly. A minute later, a third call.

A police officer was in the perfect location right at that exact moment that Sam got on the railing. The officer commanded him to get down. Sam said he didn't want to cause any trouble. He just wanted an end. But he eventually stepped down. He was alive and in the emergency room.

Everyone with the last name Harmer was already piling into cars and speeding to Twin Falls. We hit 100 mph at one point.

We waited in the emergency room for what seemed to be an hour before we got to see him. There was a printed photo on the wall of a rustic, old wooden cattle fence in the mountains that is forever burned into my mind.

Sam was heavily drugged in addition to his extreme emotional distress. He barely seemed human on that long car ride to the treatment clinic back in Boise.

With time, counseling, and medication, Sam stabilized. He met and married a wonderful woman, who we all fell in love with, and continued with his life. He taught college courses at Boise State University as an adjunct professor and life soldiered on.

He loved his wife, his seven kids, and his job. I realized how far he'd come one night when a few members of our family went out to dinner with him and he was almost like his old self. We were at the Cracker Barrel and he seemed almost identical to the real Sam I'd always known. I remarked to my wife that Sam seemed so comfortable with us and happy. Finally, my brother was starting to come back.

Little did I know that Sam had a note on his phone, right there in his pocket while we ate, detailing his plans for suicide. The note had just begun, and over the next few months he filled in the details as he thought it through.

Sam came to family dinners, spent time with his wife and kids, went to work, made vacation plans for the future, and worked with his attorney on future custody arrangements. He made plans for the future at the very time he was making plans for the end.

Friday, August 4, 2017. I like to enjoy the perks of being an internet entrepreneur, and my favorite perk is setting my own schedule. So on a Friday morning when I should have been working, I hooked the trailer up to the truck and the whole family piled in for some fun in the desert. We spent the morning dirt biking. Cole, my 7-year-old, tipped over a few times and I spent much of the morning wiping tears and being a cheerleader. We all love dirt biking as a family, so it was an excellent day with perfect weather.

As I carved dusty turns through the desert, my dear brother was four miles away, preparing to die.

It was 2 p.m. As we got in the truck to come home, I got a text from Sam. Emily read it to me while I started driving down the bumpy dirt road: "Hey brothers, a friend at work was just diagnosed with cancer. He has only one month left. Got me thinking how I've been meaning to apologize . . . for being a shitty brother ;) I mean it though. I've been through some intense life events over the past seven years and I'm seeing more clearly now how I've acted . . . On top of all of it, I was about three years into a worsening depression, as you know. Not making excuses, just explaining. I'm sorry for being distant all these years. I really do love you and always have of course. Just realizing I need to fix a few things in my life so I can move on. No need for emotional phone calls. LOL. I just wanted to say I'm sorry. Sam."

I told Emily, "Wow. That's really great. I hope he'll start feeling more like himself. Last time we went out with him he was really happy." Probably right as I said those words, he got out of his Uber and walked to the back of the parking lot at the hospital. There was a small grassy area.

It was 3:33 p.m. It took me a few minutes to figure out what to say to Sam. As I drove, I dictated a reply that Emily tapped out on my phone. "Life throws some curveballs. I'm glad you're in a better spot now. I'd love to do more with you. A little disappointed that we can't have more emotional phone calls too. ;-)" We went through a few revisions of the text to get it just right. I wanted to let him know that I loved him without sounding too emotional since Sam hates being stressed.

We got home and got the baby to sleep and I took a nap. I had slept only five minutes when I woke to a phone call. I would normally not have answered, but I saw it was one of my brothers. I was still waking up but wanted to sound awake when I answered, so I said, "Hey man. What's up?" in my most chipper voice.

He replied in a very calm, even tone: "Sam's dead . . . "

I understood the words, but had to clarify the meaning. "Where is he? Is he okay?"

" . . . He's dead."

"Wait, you mean it's already over? He's dead?"

"He's dead. He's at the emergency room in Boise."

Everyone with the last name Harmer flew into cars. 100 mph. I broke down at one point in the car, but mostly I didn't feel anything. I just couldn't be sure yet. I still felt great like I had that morning and my emotions hadn't quite caught up with the situation. I felt a little guilty talking to Emily in the car because I wasn't feeling sad and I knew I should. It still *felt* like a normal day, but I knew it wasn't.

I parked at the hospital in nearly the same space where I'd parked a year earlier when my third child, a daughter, was born. I got out of the car and started running toward the ER doors. Trying to hurry, I was annoyed by the many police cars and yellow crime tape surrounding an area near the parking lot. I ran, weaving through the maze when I suddenly stopped in my tracks as I realized that the police cars and the yellow tape were there for Sam.

I looked over, and there he was. Fortunately, I was at a distance, but there he was. I lost control. "*Why* would he do something like that?" I felt anger more than anything. The sense of waste was overpowering. The police officers asked me a few questions.

"He's been battling depression for years. Yes, he attempted suicide once in the past but that was years ago." I could only laugh when they asked if he had any enemies.

None of you will understand the pain we all felt over the ensuing days unless you've felt that same pain yourself—the pain that causes people to howl as they cry.

It was over. Sam was over, and nothing was going to go back and change it.

In writing this book, I have carefully researched the current recommendations from groups such as the American Foundation for Suicide Prevention so that I can tell this story as I lived it, but more importantly in a way that would not at all sensationalize suicide or cause harm to others. Consequently, I intentionally omitted details here that could put others at risk.

Sam didn't die from any single trauma. Many factors contributed to his death: mental illness that was only partially treated, chronic pain and medications from a recent surgery, struggles in his personal life, his unwillingness to open up to others about how he was feeling, and stress.

More than anything else, Sam's death pained me for its waste. There were so many options available to him. This could have been treated. Those at risk of suicide can call the U.S. National Suicide Prevention Lifeline at 800.273.TALK. That's 1.800.273.8255. Sam knew that, and did not reach out for help as he should have. Help was so close to him.

The solution was so simple. His brain had convinced him that he would never have a happy day ever again. Anyone who has been through difficulties knows that's not true. It was simply a problem within him that didn't allow his mind to understand that, and he could have so easily received help in the emergency room by walking in and saying, "I need help. I have no will to live." He could have called the suicide hotline. He could have told anyone who could have helped him make those decisions.

After his death, a group of Sam's friends and former students took his bucket list, which he called his "to-do list," and committed to finishing it for him. They have plowed farms in a tractor, bought a round for the bar, presented an oversized check to a charity, written books, and more. This tribute to my brother shows how his life touched me, but his life reached many others. I finally feel I can tell his story in a positive way. I can just enjoy who he was without the pain of how it ended.

About six months before his death, Sam posted on Facebook, "I'm curious to know what my friends believe about the meaning of life. I know this is a heavy subject for Facebook, but I'm genuinely curious what my friends believe deep down on a personal level.

" . . . After my midlife crisis, of sorts, I've spent the past eight years of my life searching for God and some meaning in life and I've mostly come up short . . . At the same time, I don't judge those who believe in God, in fact I envy them! Life was certainly easier for me when I was a believer . . . I didn't wake up in the middle of the night suddenly concerned about my existence and my place in the universe! This lack of faith has been terrifying for me the past few years, honestly. I've felt very alone and purposeless at times, spiritually."

I didn't feel like I could respond, or maybe I didn't feel like I should since he had lost his faith years ago and didn't like talking about it. Sam already knew what I believed. If I'm to be perfectly honest, I believe Sam struggled to find a purpose because he had ruled out any belief in the one being who gives life purpose. That's my belief, but it's not the point.

The point, and the reason it is necessary to tell this story, is this: We all need to stop setting goals in hopes of stumbling upon some kind of purpose in our lives. Go right ahead and change your college major 20 times, and I promise you'll still feel like you haven't found your "calling."

Your Career and Your Goals Are Not Your Calling

Calling? If you frame the career question that way, would *anyone* become a plumber? "Why yes, God put me on this green earth so that I could shoot human excrement through plastic pipes!" A handyman? An accountant? A mailman? A banker? Nope. We reject those because there's no way *that's* your calling in life, right? Surely *that* couldn't be it.

Certainly *we were* called to become operatic singers who delight audiences with the beauty of music, politicians who clean up corruption, or founders of nonprofits who save children in Africa, right? If we frame our life's work by viewing it as a calling, we all too often think only the most outwardly noble goals are suitable. Yet what would the world look like without plumbing, accounting, or mail delivery?

I wish Sam could know how his goals fit into the bigger picture. The value in achieving a goal is not the thing conquered, but the muscle you have grown in conquering it.

No goal will complete you.

Climb Everest, invent flying cars, have 40 kids, go to Harvard, become a senator—I don't care. You'll work yourself ragged and never find happiness.

154

That's a lesson I'm only beginning to understand. Just a couple of years ago, I was telling a friend about my business—the business I have spent years working to build and was so proud of. Somehow, I found myself saying something I didn't know I felt. I said, "Yeah, it's great, but I'm not sure how long I can keep doing this. I mean, is my whole career going to just be about sharing an endless stream of photography tips?"

The words struck me as they escaped my lips, and I knew I'd never be able to take them back. I realized something was bubbling up inside me. I wanted to take a big leap and find a new challenge. When I really thought about it, I could see that I was falling into the same trap as someone in college trying to find their "calling." The topic of my work didn't have to be meaningful.

> *I should have realized that the work was meaningful because it stretched me to learn.*

Yet I did feel that I wanted a new challenge. I was ready to sell my business. It took two years of hard work to turn the business completely passive. It was hard to see many of the things I built change to make it investable at a lower level, but I made the move. Eventually, the business did sell and Improve Photography is now an excellent and active site in great hands that are continuing to make it a great resource for photographers around the world.

My next challenge was Income School, which I was running as a separate business with my friend Ricky. The site was taking off, but at the time was still far below what my photography site had become. Making the decision to take on a new business was one of the best moves of my career. Income School has now become a staple in the internet marketing industry, and we have expanded with employees and multiple large websites about RVs, hunting, pets, and other topics in our portfolio. Plus, our YouTube channel (Income School) has absolutely blossomed.

That was the change I made in my career when I learned how short life was, but there is another change I'm only beginning to understand. I've been running scared ever since that day when I had to lay off my employees.

This morning I woke up at 3 a.m. because I had an epiphany in my sleep about how we could approach a particular problem at work. I couldn't stop thinking about the exciting problem, so I just put on my shoes and drove over to the office to get to work. I work hard because I love my work, but I've also been working out of an inner fear that it could all come crashing down again at any moment. Because of that, if I'm honest, I have a hard time connecting with other people sometimes because I'm so focused on killing it at work.

Our goals are a deeply meaningful part of who we are, but some goals will not make us any happier.

I don't hold the secrets to the universe, but I have determined a purpose in life that has helped me through difficulties and made me feel genuinely happy. Most of all, it makes me feel that every moment of my life has a meaning, no matter how mundane.

Here it is: This is my personal approach to the meaning of life that has worked for me. The purpose of life is to improve myself and my family within our sphere. It works no matter your religious beliefs. Just improve who you are, from where you currently are.

We are each born into different circumstances and families. We have different opportunities, problems, struggles, and talents. That's your sphere, and it doesn't matter where it is or what it looks like. Simply improve within it.

Again, I do not hold the secrets to the universe, but when I adopted that phrase as my running theory of the purpose of life, it helped me find meaning. For me, the purpose of life is to improve myself and my family within our sphere.

My parents are better than my grandparents were. They really are. My grandparents were wonderful people, but they struggled too. My parents saw some of those errors and they live their lives in a way that fixes those problems. They are remarkably consistent and kind people. That's the sphere I was born into, and my job is to do everything I can to take my family line a step further—to improve my family. I have my work cut out for me in a way you can't understand unless you meet my parents. That means every single night with my kids has a purpose and meaning to me. It is not about doing what is most relaxing, but what will bond us together and prepare my kids to thrive as adults.

But my purpose isn't only to improve my family's position; it is to improve myself and *my* abilities too. I need to increase my ability to do and to serve. That's why I read 60 books per year while I'm driving in the car or working out; I feel that doing so will give me an edge. That's why I have a bucket list in the first place. That's why I pray for strength every morning, and why I have a note on my phone where I write down my good turn each day, since I'm not naturally good at thinking of others as much as I should.

My brother's death caused me to reflect on what all my ambition and aspirations were even about, and in the end it has driven me to work faster, care more, and remember that life is too short to be idle for any of it. The game can end at any moment.

My goals are changing in this new season of life. I'm learning how I can set aside the "Look at me! I broke a world record in tiddlywinking!" type of goals, and change them into goals about who I am as a person. Recognizing that I've been over-focused on building an empire online to compensate for a past failure, my goals are now about building traits that make me a better person.

I'm going to climb Mount Kilimanjaro, become a hot air balloon pilot, and spend a night on a private tropical island. I am going to finish that bucket list. **But now I realize that the reason I feed work to my work energy is to help me improve myself as a person. It drives me to continually challenge myself and become stronger.**

Your work energy drives you. Mine drives me. Your work energy feeds your inner need to feel successful and helps you crush any problem in front of you. What I have learned over time is that living to work will only make me inescapably hungry for more. **Instead, I'm learning how I can use my work energy to build a muscle to improve who I am.**

Our time here on this earth is short. There are seasons in life for sprinting, and others for slowing down and living simply, but every season has a purpose. You likely will never scratch the surface of the true potential you have. But if you understand your work energy, set a goal, focus on the highest-value efforts, and groundhog the work until success, you can find yourself continually able to take on larger and more audacious goals.

Life won't be vanilla for you. You will be the one who has all the confidence to put any idea that pops into your head into action. You will be the one who never seems bothered by the little things. You will be the one who doesn't feel so trapped by work, money, or time that you can't say yes to fun. You will be the one with the happy family. You will be the one who is so excited to get up each morning that you can't sleep any longer. You will be the one being promoted at work past others who have been there longer. You will be the one people go to when they need help. You will be the strength to your family in a time of need. You will be the one who stops playing Little League. You will be the one for whom things seem to work out, and people will wonder why you're so "lucky."

So go become a goal animal. Go finish what you start, and fearlessly take on any goal.

ENDNOTES

1. https://www.gallup.com/workplace/238079/state-global-workplace-2017.aspx?g_source=link_newsv9&g_campaign=item_225752&g_medium=copy

2. https://www.researchgate.net/publication/223679624_The_resolution_solution_Longitudinal_examination_of_New_Year's_change_attempts

3. Gerber, Michael E. *The E-Myth: Why Most Small Businesses Don't Work and What to Do About It.* HarperBusiness, 1986.

4. Whitsett, David, Forrest Dolgener, and Tanjala Kole. *The Non-Runner's Marathon Trainer.* McGraw-Hill Education, 1998.

5. http://heldrich.rutgers.edu/sites/default/files/products/uploads/Work_Trends_September_2014_0.pdf

6. https://www.nature.com/articles/s41562-017-0277-0

7. Hendricks, Gay. *The Big Leap: Conquer Your Hidden Fear and Take Life to the Next Level.* HarperOne, 2010.

ABOUT THE AUTHOR

Jim Harmer is a true-blue Idahoan. He loves hunting, fishing, and camping with his family. Though he is licensed to practice law, he has been a proud blogger and YouTuber for nearly his entire professional career. He has broken two world records (longest distance traveled while playing tiddlywinks and most light orbs captured in a single photograph), and he continues to cross more items off of his bucket list every year. His current goal is to make sure his three kids—Ruger, Cole, and Faith—don't become weirdos as a result of being homeschooled.

Printed in Great Britain
by Amazon

35170604R00097